Wheels

A Passion for Collecting Cars

STUART LEUTHNER

Photographs by William Taylor

Harry N. Abrams, Inc., Publishers

Contents

Foreword

I sat down to write a few words that would properly introduce you to this remarkable book by Stuart Leuthner, and discovered almost immediately that all of my preconceptions regarding his thoughtful study of car collectors and their collections were flawed. This is not a typical formulaic ramble through several garages, not a rapturous celebration of powerful engines and shiny sheet metal, and certainly not a mere quid pro quo thank-you note to a bunch of car owners who gave the author access to their cars.

This book introduces us to a group of men who share a powerful automotive passion, and who spend an altogether disproportionate percentage of their disposable time and income on automobiles that are in one way or another special. But this book goes beyond the cars. It tells a great deal about the men themselves—how they worked and what they achieved in order to pursue the car-collecting hobby at the very highest level. It tells us how different they are from one another, and how different their collections are from one another.

We owe the world's collectors a great debt of gratitude. In assembling their collections of historic cars, military aircraft, sporting firearms, Impressionist paintings, Fabergé Easter eggs, or comic books from the 1940s, they have provided us who care about such things with living snapshots of bygone eras. We know our forebears better thanks to the collectors' obsessive zeal in seeking out and protecting the objects they love and admire.

The collector's role in protecting these wonderful things—in our case, automobiles—should never be underestimated. We take for granted the availability of a vast inventory of historic and exotic cars in the first decade of the twenty-first century, and we still cherish the wistful belief that there will be a previously undiscovered Ferrari 375 MM in that barn, but when we finally have enough money to make our own modest start on a car collection, our first really nice car will undoubtedly be one that has already passed through several other collectors' hands. Some other collector found it and restored it. Several others may have had their own seasons with it, and all that time it was being kept warm and dry for the day that one of us would come along and buy it.

Something else we take for granted these days is the fact that there is an important automotive event going on within driving distance of our homes almost any weekend of the year. This book even improves on that happy state of affairs. When we can't sleep at three o'clock on a Tuesday morning, we need only to switch on the bedside lamp, pick up our copy of Wheels, and step into any one of eleven wonderfully diverse car collections and meet their equally fascinating owners.

David E. Davis Jr.

Introduction

If the battered, cracked and broken
old stuff our ancestors tried to
get rid of now brings so much money,
think what a 1954 Oldsmobile
or a 1960 Toastmaster will bring . . .
—John Steinbeck,
Travels with Charley

In the fall of 1956, I was on my way home from

my after-school job at the drug store. It was just beginning to get dark, and the

showroom of Gillen's Lincoln-Mercury was ablaze with fluorescent light. A searchlight

threw a circling beam into the sky, lighting up low, scudding clouds. I was just about to

cross Delaware Avenue when I realized what was going on. The new cars had arrived.

A light rain began to fall as I hurried over to the dealership. Front and center

in the showroom window was a flashy red and white Mercury Montclair hardtop.

Behind that, a yellow and black station wagon. Nice, but what really got my attention

was a vision in lavender—a Lincoln Premiere convertible.

Gordon Apker

Gordon Apker's first vehicle was a 1922 Dodge truck. "It was given to me by a neighbor," he says, "for cleaning out their chicken coops. I was twelve, and my father wouldn't let me drive it on a real road, so I cleared away some trees and drove it around our property." His next ride was a 1936 Ford four-door sedan that he bought from another neighbor for $10, making payments of $2.50 for four months. "It was a pretty nice car," Apker says, "but I really wanted a convertible, so I cut the top of the car off with a hacksaw." He laughs, "It didn't take me long to realize the need for a metal top on a sedan. The car sagged so bad in the middle that the doors had to be tied together to keep them shut." To combat the elements, Apker built a frame out of two-by-fours and covered it with a green Army tent. It's a shame he never took a photograph of the Ford because it must have been one ugly automobile.

"Some friends and myself would go what we called 'stump jumping' on the logging roads," Apker says. "We would build a ramp with logs and dirt and then go over it as fast as we could get the car going. One time we actually landed on a stump, and that was the end of that car."

Apker grew up in Mukileto, a small town north of Seattle. His father was a millwright for the Scott Paper Company. "My dad had three brothers," he says. "None of them reached fifty. Each time one died, we inherited his family. We raised our own food—cows for our milk, chickens, a large vegetable garden. We didn't have indoor plumbing until 1952."

Although money was scarce, Apker has fond memories of his childhood. "I had," he says, "one of those rare families where the parents actually liked each other. They were married sixty-six years. My brother and sister were older, so I kind of grew up as an only child. All I saw was their taillights in the distance."

When he was fourteen, Apker went to work in a gas station. "I would go down to the Texaco station, hang around, and offer to do anything—wash the owner's car, sweep up, whatever. He must have felt sorry for me because he gave me a job. I loved it because I was around cars. When I was in high school, a buddy of mine had a 1940 Mercury coupe. He had money but didn't know anything about mechanics. I didn't have any money, but I did know how to work on cars.

We put a 1954 Cadillac motor—with three carburetors—and a 1939 LaSalle tranny in that Merc."

Apker shrugs, "I made a deal with him that if he ever wanted to sell the car I would get first crack. I think it was during my third year of college he called and said he was going to sell it for $1,500. He might as well have said $10 million."

In 1962, Apker enrolled at Pacific Lutheran University, a liberal-arts school located in Tacoma, Washington. "I was studying to be a Lutheran minister," he says. "I was still working in a service station, but I left Texaco and began working at a Veltex station."

Now that he was a college student, Apker stepped up to a 1955 Chrysler New Yorker two-door hardtop. "Boy," he says, "I thought I was styling. I put on baby moon hubcaps and lowered the car."

Coming home from a date, Apker drove across some railroad tracks, and the lowering block was ejected from one of the springs. "The car," Apker says, "was riding with one corner high. It looked foolish, and I didn't want anybody on campus to see me. It was the middle of the night, but I had the keys to the gas station, so I put the car up on the lift and removed the other three blocks. That was the end of my lowered Chrysler."

Apker met Claudia Smith at Pacific Lutheran, and they were married in the

Previous page: Gordon Apker in his Veltex shop coat. While he was attending college, Apker worked at a Veltex station to pay his tuition. The oil company went out of business in 1964, but Apker helps to keep the Veltex flame alive.

Left: A 1931 SJ Duesenberg Roadster (front) and a 1933 Cadillac Dual Cowl Phaeton. During the 1930s, Errett Lobban Cord purchased bankrupt Duesenberg Inc. of Indianapolis. Cord then commissioned Frank Duesenberg to design a high-speed touring automobile that would be an American alternative to Europe's finest automobiles. In 1932, a supercharged version of the Model J, the Model SJ, was offered. Duesenberg claimed a top speed of 129 mph.

Above: A pink 1956 Cadillac Eldorado from Apker's collection provided an attention-getting window display at his Seattle Shakey's pizza restaurants in the 1980s.

Right: Apker has assembled an eclectic mix. Classics, hot rods, one-of-a-kind cars, toys, collectibles—they are all here. The gold F-88 was Oldsmobile's attempt to create its own version of the Corvette.

Below: A toy from Apker's collection.

spring of his junior year, a move that did not sit at all well with the school. "The counselor," he says, "for the kids who were going to be ministers called me into his office and had a fit. Lutheran ministers could, of course, get married, but he told me that I was going to be distracted. That made me so mad I changed my major to become a juvenile probation officer."

The program required Apker to attend court twice a week. He quickly decided that a career in juvenile probation was not for him. "A buddy of mine wanted to go into the FBI," Apker says. "I thought that sounded good, but it meant putting in an extra year to pick up some courses. That was 1964. Claudia and I were living in student housing, and money was so tight that she had to drop out of school and work for the phone company. The Chrysler was long gone—I totaled it a week after I got married. I was driving a $50 1941 Oldsmobile and working at the Veltex station."

Later that year, a few days after Claudia discovered she was pregnant, the Veltex Oil Company went out of business. "The owner handed me twenty bucks and told me we were closing up," he recalls. With a baby on the way and tuition to pay, Apker needed another job. On his way home, he stopped at an all-night Texaco station. "They needed somebody for the midnight-to-eight shift," he says. "The problem with that was, I had a class that started at eight. I cut a deal with the manager where I could leave fifteen minutes early."

With no time to change, Apker would arrive at his Greek class in his Texaco Star outfit, reeking of Fire Chief gasoline and Medium 5 grease. "Pacific was a private school," Apker says, "and most of the kids were from money. I think back to what I must have looked and smelled like."

A 1947 Delahaye coupe built by Lagenthal of Switzerland. In 1933, Delahaye, a company known for building dependable, but undistinguished, automobiles, made the decision to add luxury cars to its product line. Delahayes were outfitted with some of the most fanciful bodywork ever seen on automobiles, created by a who's-who of the world's finest coachbuilders. The frog hood ornament is especially tasty.

After six weeks on his new job, Apker had an experience that would have a dramatic effect on his future. "There was a Standard station across the street," he says. "The guy who worked there would meet me in the middle of the street at 3:30 A.M., and we would talk. One night he didn't come out, and I found him tied up in the back of the station. He'd been robbed."

Apker was rethinking the risky night shift when a friend, Greg Hinton, called and told him he knew somebody who was opening a Shakey's pizza parlor in Tacoma. "He told me they were looking for people," Apker says. "I had always worked in gas stations—cold, rain, oil, grease—and had never considered anything else. The thought of working inside where it was warm and clean sounded very agreeable, so I took the job."

The combination of great pizza and a lively atmosphere made Shakey's a success. Described "as much like a pub as a pizza parlor," the restaurant featured a piano player cranking out Dixieland jazz and a spirited staff, dressed in striped vests and straw hats, doling out the tasty pies. After working at Shakey's for three months, Apker was promoted to assistant manager. "The job paid $425 a month," Apker says, "which I thought at that time was a fortune."

Four months before Apker's graduation, the three partners who owned the restaurant had a falling out. Two of them bought out the third, who then decided to open his own Shakey's. "He asked me," Apker says, "if I would like to be his assistant manager."

Apker said yes, and, being a "stand-up guy," he told the remaining two owners that he was going to work for their ex-partner. "I gave them two months' notice," he says, laughing. "They fired me the next day."

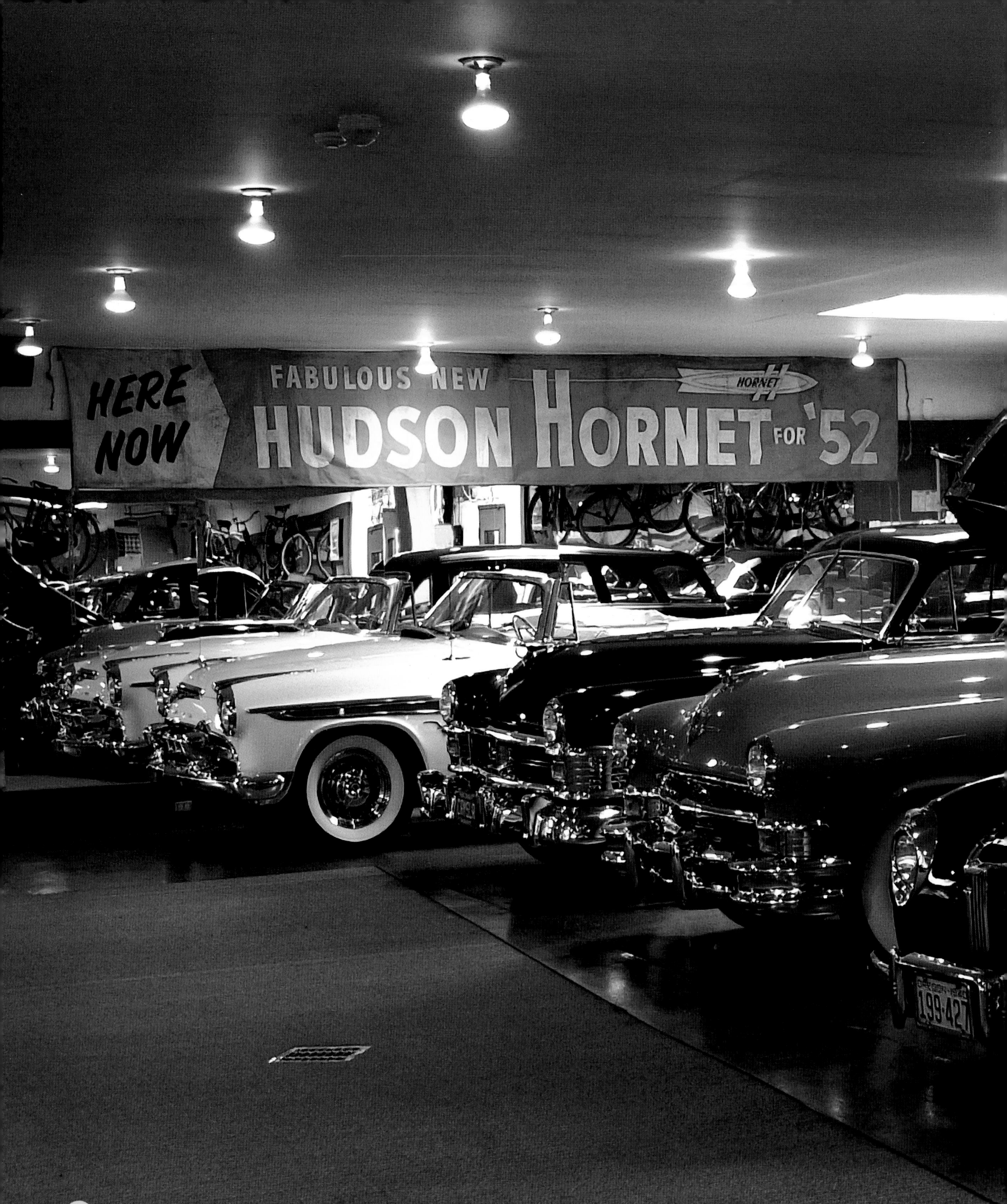
HERE NOW
FABULOUS NEW
HUDSON HORNET FOR '52
HORNET

The white car in this lineup is a rare 1955 DeSoto Fireflite convertible, one of only 775 examples built. It was equipped with a 200-horsepower V-8. Priced to compete with Pontiac and Oldsmobile, DeSoto was launched in 1928. A short thirty-three years later, the marque would be relegated to history.

By then Apker had a daughter, Kimberly, born in 1966. Since it would be at least six weeks before the new store would open, he needed a paycheck. His father managed to get him a temporary job on a maintenance crew at Scott Paper. "I was driving to Everett to work at the paper company, driving back to attend classes, and helping to get the restaurant ready to open. It was hectic."

Finally, the restaurant was ready to open. "Then," Apker says, "the owner's wife leaves him. While he was trying to put his marriage back together, I found myself in charge of the opening. I couldn't even go to my graduation because I had to work dinner."

Impressed with Apker's initiative, his boss told him that he would give him 20 percent of the business if Apker could come up with $3,000. "There was no way," Apker says, "that I could come up with that kind of money, so I called up Greg Hinton, the guy who got me my first job at Shakey's. He loaned me the money."

In 1969, Apker and his partner opened their second restaurant, and a year later, a third. "By then," Apker says, "We had equalized our shares and were fifty-fifty owners."

In 1970, Claudia and Gordon's second daughter, Leisha, was born. That same year, the partners opened a Shakey's in Anchorage. "In those days," Apker says, "we had to do about $300,000 a year in volume per store to break even. That first year, the Anchorage store did over $1 million We opened a second store."

Now that he was making money, Apker began to collect cars. "I bought a 1947 Oldsmobile," he says. "I guess you could call it a drivable collectible because I drove it every day to work. That car is still in my collection."

He continues, "My first real collectible automobile was a 1936 Auburn. When

Apker's re-creation of a Veltex gas station, complete with the pump from the original location where he worked. His collection of Veltex petroliana is amazing. There is even a vintage condom in the register in case the attendant gets lucky. The 1936 Ford sedan delivery is painted to represent a Veltex shop truck. Lettered on the truck's side is the company's slogan, "Great lube jobs since 1944."

I was a kid, one of my uncles had a red Auburn cabriolet with outside pipes. At the time he probably paid almost nothing for it, but I thought he must be rich."

Apker's next acquisitions included a 1942 Lincoln Continental, a 1933 Oldsmobile, and a 1948 Pontiac hearse. "I'm not sure what the hearse was all about," he says, shaking his head. "All of those cars have gone away."

During 1978, Apker began to buy what he describes as "more serious stuff." "Prior to that," he says, "the most expensive car I bought was probably ten grand. An old fellow in Portland wanted to sell me his 1929 Duesenberg. There was no way at that time I could justify paying that kind of money, but, for some reason, he wanted me to pay him $1 down and $22,000 for ten years. That was just great."

"I bought the core of my collection between 1979 and 1984. The Shakey's restaurants were paying for themselves, and I had a ton of cash in CDs. For a lot of other people the economy was terrible, so cars were falling from the sky because they needed money." He laughs, "When the word got out that I was buying cars, my phone never stopped ringing."

By 1980, Apker and his partner had fifteen stores, and they were both taking home some serious money. "Then, the economy hiccupped," Apker says. "He got nervous and I bought him out."

Once in a while, Apker would run into his college classmates. "They'd stop by the restaurants," he says, "or I'd see them at some event. They were wearing suits, carrying briefcases, and driving company cars. I smelled like oregano, and I think they felt sorry for me."

As his restaurants began to grow in number, however, Apker began to notice a change in their attitude. "They began to ask me, 'How many restaurants do you have now?' A number of my old college buddies ended up working for me."

By early 1984, Apker had forty-five stores, located in Washington, Oregon, and Alaska. He also opened Monarch Foods, a wholesale food company. "Instead of buying from suppliers, I bought from manufacturers and supplied my own stores. I also began to supply other pizza restaurants, taco stands, places like that."

Supplying the competition put Apker in an enviable position. "My manager," Apker says, "would notice that Round Table Pizza in such-and-such district was doing great volume. We were selling them Coke syrup and could compute what

Few automobiles have had the impact that the Cord 810 did when it was introduced in the fall of 1936. Designed by Gordon Buehrig, the "baby" Duesenberg's hood was low, its headlights were raised or lowered by cranks on the dash, it had no running boards, shifting was accomplished by a lever on the steering column, and it had front-wheel drive. In 1937, the year that Apker's 812 Sportsman was built, supercharging had been added, along with chrome exhaust pipes similar to those used on the Duesenberg SJs. Alas, problems with the cars, both in production and quality, turned potential customers away. Not only was the car prone to vapor lock, leaks, and transmission problems, the front-wheel-drive system was extremely complex and required a talented mechanic for maintenance and repair. As sales waned, Auburn began to close down unprofitable operations, including Cord. The last example of one of America's most innovative automobiles was built in 1940. The original owner of Apker's car was bandleader Paul Whiteman.

The Chrysler D'Elegance was designed by Virgil Exner, the man who "saved" Chrysler in the 1950s. In 1954, K. T. Keller, Chrysler Motor Corporation's chairman, distressed over sagging sales, promoted Exner to director of styling and ordered him to bring Chrysler back into contention. Exner had already been exploring designs with the Italian firm Carrozzeria Ghia, and during the next fifteen years Ghia would produce a series of handcrafted "idea cars" under Exner's direction. The D'Elegance, built in 1953, was the first car to use the futuristic "gun-sight" taillights that would appear on the 1955–56 Imperials. Tom McCahill, the writer who turned car testing into an art form in the pages of *Mechanix Illustrated*, referred to them as "sparrow-strainers." The D'Elegance had no trunk, so it was equipped with a set of custom-fitted luggage, stored behind the back seat. A spare tire, mounted on the back deck, was deployed by pushing a button on the dash. Apker demonstrated the feature to us, and, although it seems to be a rather overblown method of delivering a spare tire, it is impressive.

we call gallonage. In a pizza restaurant, 20 percent of your sales are soft drinks. Once I knew a store was doing well, I would put up a Shakey's next to them. Some of the chains eventually found out I owned Monarch Foods, and we lost a few. That was fine."

Apker was on the board of Hunt International Company, the group that now owned Shakey's. "I was the sole representative of the Shakey's team, and it was obvious they had no interest in Shakey's. I had also figured out that if you are a franchise, you are under the thumb of the franchiser." He and two friends who owned Shakey's in Sacramento discovered that the Hunt brothers—in big trouble because of shenanigans in the silver market—were being pressed by their bank to sell some of their holdings. "We met with the bank in 1984," Apker says. "They were glad to get anything off their books, so we bought Shakey's for $17 million. At that time, there were close to six hundred restaurants in the United States and abroad."

The bank had one stipulation—Shakey's headquarters had to remain in Dallas. Since Apker was running a large operation in Seattle, and also put up the money, he stayed where he was and his partners relocated to Dallas.

In 1988, Apker's partners received a phone call from the Shakey's franchise in Singapore. "They wanted to buy everything outside of the United States and Canada," Apker says. "The price was right, so we sold it to them. They ultimately bought all of my stores and the wholesale food company. That was February of 1989, and I walked away."

In 1993 Apker and his wife were divorced, and he moved to Scottsdale.

One of the two F-88 prototypes produced by GM was scheduled to be driven in the 1954 Macy's Thanksgiving parade. The car's engine caught on fire in the staging area and, when nobody could find the hood release, the car burned to the ground. Chevrolet, having problems selling the Corvette, convinced GM to abandon the F-88 program. This car went through a series of owners, including Harley Earl and E. L. Cord—yes, that Cord—before ending up in Apker's collection. Automobile styling in the 1950s was heavily influenced by the aircraft industry, and the F-88's dashboard would be right at home in the cockpit of a jet fighter.

After a couple of years in the warm Arizona sun, he moved back to Seattle. A friend introduced him to Janet Erickson at the unlimited hydro races, and they were married in 2000.

Since selling Shakey's, Apker has been associated with a variety of ventures, including real estate, but he still manages to spend time with his cars. He keeps his collection in a barn—a very nice barn. Commanding a postcard view of Washington's Puget Sound, the 17,000-square-foot compound is home to a remarkable collection of automobiles and memorabilia.

"The barn was built in 1899," Apker says, "by the founder of the Alaska Steamship Line. He collected exotic birds on a very large scale. When I bought the compound, in 1969, one of the buildings still contained the original roosts and cages."

Apker used the buildings to store his growing collection, but a wind storm convinced him to turn the place into the showplace it is today. "In 1972," he says, "a big tree blew over and landed on the roof. A short time later I began the restoration, and a few years later I built the house."

On my tour through Apker's barn, I was fascinated by the eclectic mix he has assembled—classics, hot rods, one-of-a-kind cars, toys, art, collectibles. A beautifully restored 1936 Ford three-window, powered by an Eddy Meyer warmed-up flathead, sits next to a rare 1955 DeSoto Fireflite; only 775 of the hemi-powered ragtops were built. Today, very few survive.

Apker's first "collectible" purchase, his 1947 Oldsmobile, is a study in aftermarket accessories. In addition to rear Venetian blinds, the straight-eight-powered Dynamic Deluxe Club Sedan is fitted with a compass, a clock, a fan, and an automatic cigarette lighter.

To celebrate the years he toiled in gas stations, Apker has re-created a Veltex station, complete with a pump from the original location where he worked. His collection of Veltex petroliana is amazing, as is his attention to detail. There's even a vintage condom in the register in case the attendant gets lucky.

In another room, we come upon a rather brutal-looking bright yellow sports car, with a large number "8" painted on the door. It is one of Max Balchowsky's legendary "Old Yallar" racers.

Balchowsky was a seat-of-the-pants genius who, with help from his wife, Ina, built a series of nine cars he originally called "Old Yeller." He was forced to change

the spelling when the Disney studio protested. Driven by Balchowsky and other famous drivers, including Dan Gurney and Carroll Shelby, the V-8-powered cars routinely beat the best European road racers in the 1950s.

Apker's "Old Yallar VIII" was built from a wrecked Jaguar XKE. Balchowsky had planned to use it as a street car but sold it when he lost interest in the project. Until recently, Apker raced the car in vintage events. He had to quit because of problems with his vision.

"That's a very fast car," Apker says, "and I won a lot of races. But, I got a tear in my retina. The doctors told me that if I hit my head really hard, I could lose my vision. It's not worth it."

Following Apker into another room, I was confronted with a sculpted sports coupe. Painted a rich maroon, the handsome car's sloping roofline was accentuated by full cutout wheel wells framing elegant spoked wheels. I had absolutely no idea what I was looking at, but I did recognize the "gun-sight" taillights used on the 1955 and 1956 Chrysler Imperials.

Obviously I was not the first to express ignorance because Apker, sensing my bewilderment, immediately said, "It's a Chrysler D'Elegance. One of the 'idea cars' designed by Virgil Exner and built by Ghia in 1953."

Long before Lee Iacocca convinced the government to loan the Chrysler Motor Corporation $1.5 billion, Virgil Exner almost single-handedly saved the auto

builder from disaster. During the early 1950s, Chrysler was in big trouble. While Ford and General Motors were offering the public longer and lower, Chrysler was selling stodgy. The auto maker's efforts were described by the motoring press as following "a three-box design philosophy—one box sitting on two boxes." K. T. Keller, Chrysler's chairman, smugly declared that his company's styling "won't knock your hat off, but neither will getting in one of our cars."

Headroom was not what American car buyers were looking for. During the winter of 1952–53, Chrysler Motor Corporation's sales slipped into third place, behind Ford. By the end of the 1954 season, Plymouth was in fifth place, outsold not only by its traditional rivals, Ford and Chevrolet, but also Buick and Pontiac.

Finally realizing that something dramatic had to be done, Keller promoted Exner, who at the time headed Chrysler's Advanced Styling Studio, to director of styling, with an order to bring the company back into contention.

Exner had already been exploring future designs with the Italian firm Carrozzeria Ghia. This relationship not only helped to reverse Chrysler's fortunes but created what became known as the "Forward Look," a style that would influence an entire generation of automobile designers.

Virgil M. Exner was born in 1909, in Ann Arbor, Michigan. Fascinated with cars and art, he collected automobile catalogues from the time he wa seven and studied art at Notre Dame. At the end of his sophomore year,

Hot rodders love chrome. The engine in the McGowan Brothers' hi-boy is typical of the powerplants that were installed in many hot rods during the 1950s. The Ford flathead V-8 engine first appeared in 1932. Constant improvements made the engine more reliable and powerful until 1953, the last year the flathead was used in Ford automobiles. Even though Detroit replaced the engine with the overhead-valve V-8, the flathead has remained a favorite with hot rodders. Almost as soon as the engine appeared, manufacturers began producing bolt-on speed equipment for the flathead to make it go faster—or at least look faster. Dual and triple manifolds, high-compression heads (like the Edmond's on the McGowans' car), racing cam shafts, and lots of chrome goodies—the list is endless.

Exner ran short of funds and had to leave school.

The young designer went to work for a South Bend art studio, illustrating automotive ads and catalogues. A few years later he took his portfolio to General Motors, and Harley Earl hired him to work in the Pontiac design studio.

In 1938, Raymond Loewy was looking for talent to work on the Studebaker account and offered to double Exner's salary from $400 a month to $800. Exner left GM and spent more than a decade working in Loewy's South Bend studios, but it was not an amicable relationship.

Although Exner was the primary designer of Studebaker's 1947 Starlight Coupe, Loewy believed that everything designed in his studio was the result of his own genius and gave no credit to any of his associates. As time went by, it was reported that Exner and Loewy grew to despise each other.

Fed up with Loewy's ego, Exner quit and went to work for Chrysler. In 1951, he began the fifteen-year relationship with Ghia that would result in a series of handcrafted "idea cars." These included the K-310, the C-200, the DeSoto Adventurer, the Falcon, the Dodge Firearrow, and the Chrysler D'Elegance.

If he was going to radically change Chrysler's image, Exner realized he needed time—it takes three years to create a new model car. His first "Forward Look" designs for 1955 were new, but not that new. They were certainly not the dumpy cars of the past, but they relied more on three-tone paint jobs, "gun-sight" tail-lights, and "Flair Fashion" styling than on revolutionary design.

In 1956, modest fins and big horsepower continued the erosion of Chrysler's earlier image, but it would be in 1957, with his second-generation "Forward Look," that Exner's vision would come to fruition. The long, low, wedge-shaped Chrysler New Yorkers, DeSoto Firedomes, Dodge Crown Royals, Imperial Crown Southamptons, and Plymouth Furys, with their soaring, attention-getting fins, were an instant hit. "We wanted," Exner explained, "to give our cars an eager, poised-for-action look that we feel is the natural and functional shape of automobiles."

Customers crowded Chrysler's showrooms, often lining up at the doors before they opened, and Plymouth quickly moved solidly back into third position. It is hard to believe that the 1957 Chrysler products had any connection with the cars the company was selling only a few years earlier.

Exner, considered to be a genius, became Chrysler's first vice-president of design, overseeing a staff of more than three hundred designers, engineers, and support personnel. Resenting Exner's success, Raymond Loewy sent him a model car with enormous, cartoonlike fins, along with a letter deriding Exner's designs.

Success is a fickle mistress, especially in the automobile business. Exner's facelifts for 1958 were criticized as too little, and in 1959, as too much. Quality also became a major issue. Chrysler products were plagued with a litany of problems, including rattles, leaks, and premature rust.

A heart attack in 1956 took Exner out of the loop during the early development of the 1960 and 1961 models. This unfortunate turn of events was compounded when Chrysler vice-president William E. Newberg became convinced that Chevrolet and Ford were going to downsize their cars for 1962. He insisted that Exner follow suit, even though the designer told him the cars would "look like hell." The truncated results were a disaster, and, when the new full-sized Chevrolets and Fords rolled out, Chrysler's executives realized they had been had.

Somebody had to take the fall for management's mistake, and Exner was demoted from vice-president to consultant. He left Chrysler and, assisted by his son, Virgil Jr., opened his own industrial-design studio in Birmingham, Michigan.

Exner designed a series of boats for Buhler, Brunswick, Pacemaker, Mathews, Bristol Yachts, and Riva, and explored design proposals for "updated" versions of classic cars of the 1930s. Drawings of his modern-day Stutz, Duesenberg, Packard, and Mercer concepts were published in a 1963 issue of *Esquire*.

In 1966, Exner announced that he would build a neo-classic Duesenberg. He had actually begun to take orders, but the project abruptly ended after only one car was built when a major financial backer pulled out.

A rather overblown version of Exner's Stutz was produced with help from John DeLorean. Built in Italy but based on American cars, and powered by American V-8s, the Blackhawk Stutz was popular with the show-business crowd. Liberace, Isaac Hayes, Dean Martin, Willie Nelson, and Lucille Ball were among the car maker's customers; Elvis bought five. The Italian factory produced approximately fifty cars a year until production ceased in the early 1990s.

Virgil Exner died on December 22, 1973, in Birmingham, Michigan. The last car he owned was a 1973 Oldsmobile.

"I've always liked the concept cars that Exner created for Chrysler," Apker

Clive Cussler

Pitt thanked the airport maintenance man who had given him a lift from the terminal area. Glancing around to see that he wasn't observed, he took a small transmitter from his coat pocket and issued a series of voice commands that closed down the security systems and opened a side door that looked as if it hadn't swung on its hinges for thirty years. He entered and stepped onto a polished concrete floor that held nearly three dozen gleaming, classic automobiles, an antique airplane, and a turn-of-the-century railroad car. He paused and stared fondly at the chassis of a French Talbot-Lago sports coupe that was in an early stage of reconstruction. The car had been nearly destroyed in an explosion, and he was determined to restore the twisted remains to their previous elegance and beauty.

— CYCLOPS (1986)

The mighty fins of the 1957 Lincoln Premiere convertible. Lincoln described the fins as "crisp, canted rear blades," and invited prospective customers to drive the car for a weekend with no obligation to buy. An ad for the promotion promised, "With a Lincoln parked in your driveway, you can compare its long, low, clean-lined kind of styling with that of any other fine car in your neighborhood."

After high school, Cussler enrolled at Pasadena City College, but two years later the Korean War began to heat up. He and a couple of friends enlisted in the Air Force, and Cussler spent the next three years in Hawaii, working as a mechanic and flight engineer in the Military Air Transport Service. He spent his time alternating between the oily innards of Boeing C-97 Stratocruisers and skin-diving in Oahu's crystalline bays and coves.

"We were diving fanatics," Cussler says. "There was little in the way of equipment in the early 1950s. My first mask was a rather strange affair, with two snorkels that were equipped with Ping-Pong balls to keep the water out. My first fins resembled bedroom slippers with flaps."

Wanting to go beyond the limits of snorkels, Cussler and his friends ordered what they were told was the first tank and regulator to be shipped to Hawaii. "We took turns diving off a reef in twenty feet of water," he says. "Those were the days before scuba certification by qualified instructors, and it was a wonder we didn't suffer any number of diving maladies."

Returning to California in 1954, Cussler bought an XK-120 Jaguar, married Barbara Knight, and with a friend, Dick Klein, opened a gas station. "Clive and Dick's Petrol

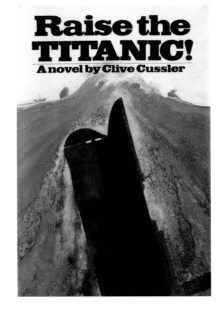

Emporium," Cussler says, "was located just off the San Bernardino Freeway. We had a three-wheeled Harley-Davidson motorcycle and would respond to all sorts of terrible accidents with a toolbox. Our job was to take the doors off so the medical folks could get to the bodies. Of all my experiences, that gas station is the one I should write about. We were held up, burglarized, short changed, cheated, fleeced, and vandalized." When it became obvious that Mobil was not interested in letting their station grow, the partners sold the business.

Needing a new career, Cussler found his first niche. "Advertising and I were meant for each other," he says, smiling. "A devious mind, combined with an industrious talent for innuendo, duplicity, and hokum." After three years as an advertising manager for Richie's Lido Market in Newport Beach, Cussler opened an advertising agency. "My partner," he says, "Leo Bestgen, was an illustrator, and we had a lot of fun. But, we were two young guys, full of ideas. Leo wanted to concentrate on illustration, and I wanted to go to work for a big-name ad agency."

Cussler got a copywriting job with a Los Angeles agency, and by the mid-1960s had worked his way up to creative director at Darcy McManus, one of the country's most prestigious agencies. A television commercial Cussler

In 1956, Studebaker launched a quartet of sporty Hawks: the Golden Hawk, the Silver Hawk, the Sky Hawk, and the Power Hawk. A year later, only the Golden Hawk and the Silver Hawk were available. The 1957 Studebaker Golden Hawk, sporting a set of obligatory fins, featured a 275-horsepower V-8 engine, equipped with a Paxton supercharger. The blower provided "extra power the instant you need it."

produced while he was at Darcy won an award at the Cannes Film Festival.

Cussler was commuting between Los Angeles and his home in Costa Mesa. Barbara was working nights as a dispatcher for the local police department. After feeding the kids—by then they had Teri, Dirk, and Dana—in the evening, Cussler found himself "with nobody to talk to," so he decided to write a book.

"I didn't have the great American novel burning inside me," Cussler says, "or an Aunt Fanny, who came across the prairie in a covered wagon, to chronicle. I thought it might be fun to try and produce a paperback adventure series."

Drawing on his experience in marketing, Cussler analyzed the successful series heroes to discover what made them work. Beginning with Edgar Allen Poe's Inspector Dumas, he studied them all: Sherlock Holmes, Bulldog Drummond, Sam Spade, Phillip Marlowe, Mike Hammer, and James Bond.

Cussler realized that his protagonist had to be different if his work had any chance of being noticed. "Bond was really hot at that time," he says, "and I knew that any similarity to him would be a dead end." The result was marine engineer Dirk Pitt and his National Underwater and Marine Agency (NUMA).

"I was looking for a good, tough name," Cussler says. "My son, Dirk, was six months old, and my desk was in his room. He would be sleeping in his crib while I was writing, so I decided to use his name."

"Perhaps I can help clear the air." The new voice came soft but firm with an authoritative resonance.

Koski stiffened in his chair and turned to a figure who leaned negligently against the doorway—a tall, well-proportioned figure. The oak-tanned face, the hard, almost cruel features, the penetrating green eyes suggested that this wasn't a man to step on. Clad in a blue Air Force flight jacket and uniform, watchful yet detached, he offered Koski a condescending grin.

"Ah, there you are," Hennewell said loudly. "Commander Koski, may I present Major Dirk Pitt. Special Projects Director for NUMA."
— ICEBERG (1975)

The fledgling author finished his first book, *Pacific Vortex*, in 1968. At his wife's suggestion, he left the ad agency and went to work for a Newport Beach dive shop so he could concentrate on his writing.

When business was slow, Cussler would peck away at a portable typewriter on a card table behind the counter. He finished *Mediterranean Caper* in a little over a year, and as an added bonus became a certified diver.

Cussler briefly returned to advertising, but he was hooked on writing, even though he had yet to sell a chapter. Copies of *Pacific Vortex* sent to numerous publishers resulted in a steady flow of rejection letters. He thought he

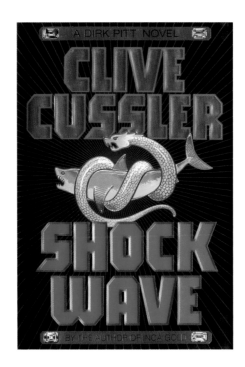

might have more luck if he had a literary agent, but that search was also coming up empty since he had no track record.

Finally, Cussler had an art director at his agency create a letterhead for a bogus movie screenwriting agency and then wrote a letter, on the letterhead, recommending himself to Peter Lampack at the William Morris Agency in New York. Lampack liked *Mediterranean Caper* and agreed to represent Cussler.

Now committed to a full-time writing career, Cussler also wanted a change of scenery. Fed up with Southern California smog and traffic, he sold his house, bought a new 1969 Mercury sedan, and hitched it to a tent trailer, and the Cussler clan hit the road for parts unknown.

"I figured," he says, "it was almost impossible to starve to death in the United States." They ended up in Estes Park, Colorado, and Cussler spent the next year writing *Iceberg*.

With his savings running low, and nobody interested in publishing any of his books, Cussler bought a house in Denver and reluctantly went back to writing advertising copy. After two years, he left the agency, withdrew to his unfinished basement, and began to work on *Raise the Titanic!*

Why the *Titanic*? "When I'm asked to speak to writing classes," Cussler says, "they will ask me where I get my ideas. I tell them it starts with the basic concept. There had already been several excellent books about the *Titanic*—Walter Lord's *A Night to Remember*, and Geoffrey Marcus's *The Maiden Voyage*—so there was obvious interest in the subject."

He continues, "My idea was, What if they raised the *Titanic*? Why? There is something on the ship of value. Who could afford to do it? The government. Why

Above: The Ninety-Eight was Oldsmobile's top model, and in 1958 this purple ragtop cost $4,300. The continental kit, a popular accessory in the 1950s, extended what were already large cars another two or three feet and made access to the trunk extremely difficult.

Left: God is in the details.

In 1958, Harley Earl was in the twilight of his career. Chrysler's Virgil Exner had out-finned him with his second generation "Forward Look," and Earl was desperately looking for something new. His answer was chrome—lots of it! Buick resurrected the Limited, a name that had not been used since the 1930s, for its top-of-the-line

midnight-black 1936 Cadillac V-16, the automotive equivalent of a battleship, was originally owned by Admiral Ernest J. King, Chief of Naval Operations and Commander in Chief of the U.S. Fleet during World War II.

In their time, town cars were extremely expensive, both to purchase and to maintain. According to Cussler, nothing has changed.

"I was having the 1938 Packard V-12 restored," he says. "It was missing the generator." After searching numerous flea markets, junkyards, and classified ads for more than two years, he finally found one.

"The generator's owner wanted $1,600." Cussler says, grimacing. "The thing was a basket case, and I asked him, rather sarcastically, 'Isn't that a little steep?' The guy looked at me, shrugged, and said, just as sarcastically, 'Well, I guess you could keep on looking.'"

Cussler laughs, "He made his point. I capitulated, bought the generator, and had to spend another $600 to overhaul it. I think it was about then that I decided to concentrate on 1950s convertibles. They used to say that when you bought one of these big chrome barges, you received your own zip code."

The high-end 1950s cars that are represented in Cussler's collection were the vehicles that helped Americans roar away from the war years and into the space age. They certainly expressed Detroit's vision of

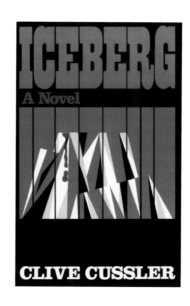

prosperity—excessive size, outrageous horsepower, and copious amounts of chrome.

And yet, in an overblown way, these vehicles are enchanting. When I was growing up, these big-ticket leviathans were the crown jewels in dealers' showrooms. They were definitely not the kind of car my father drove—he was a four-door-family-car kind of guy. Chrysler 300s, Lincoln Continentals, Olds Ninety-Eights, Packard Caribbeans, Buick Roadmasters, and Cadillac Eldorado Biarritzes were driven by doctors, bank presidents, lawyers, and my Uncle Will, who owned a department store.

So far none of the ragtops have appeared in a Cussler book, but I would not rule out the possibility. I can see Pitt behind the wheel of a 1959 Pontiac Bonneville, a shapely number in the passenger seat, pursued by an ominous black sedan. With three carburetors feeding high-test fuel to the Bonneville's throbbing three hundred horses, the bad guys would not have a chance!

Among the classics, town cars, and 1950s cars, one finds the occasional maverick: a 1938 Harley-Davidson motorcycle, complete with sidecar (a gift from Cussler's wife), and a real oddball, a 1948 Tatra. Built in Czechoslovakia, the Tatra has been described as a "customized Volkswagen." It is another one of those "beautiful-ugly" cars.

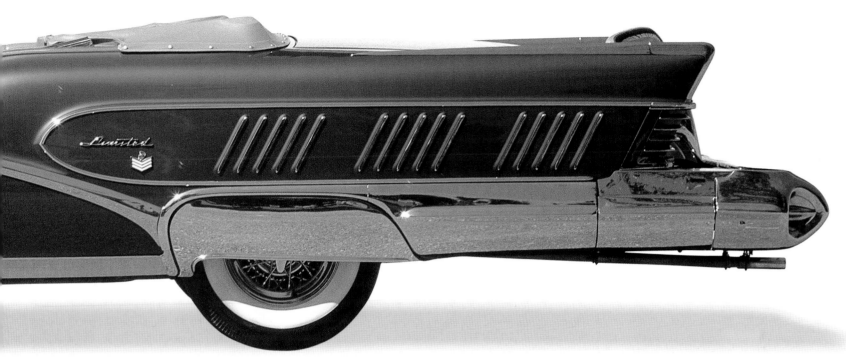

model. In addition to an abundance of brightwork, the Limited featured Twin-Tower taillights and the studded Dynastar grille. Only 839 convertibles were built, and less than two dozen of them are still known to exist.

In one aisle, a bright red Allard crouches. Describing the Allard, *Road & Track* magazine stated, "One can, if he's so inclined, label the Allard the most consistently successful hot rod of all time." Another writer called it, "a car combining one thousand pounds of horsepower within five hundred pounds of chassis."

"Do you actually drive this thing," she asked.

"I do." he answered solemnly.

"What do you call it?"

"A J2X Allard," Pitt answered, holding open a tiny aluminum door.

"It looks old."

"Built in England in 1952, at least twenty-five years before you were born. Installed with big American V-8 engines. Allards cleaned up at the sports-car races until the Mercedes 300 SL coupes came along."

Maeve slipped into the Spartan cockpit, her legs stretched out nearly parallel to the ground. She noticed that the dashboard did not sport a speedometer, only four engine gauges and tachometer.

"Will it get us where we're going?" she asked with some trepidation.

"Not in drawing-room comfort, but she comes close to the speed of sound," he said laughing.

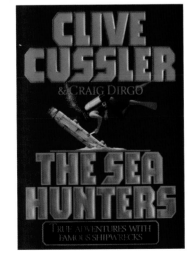

"It doesn't even have a top."

"I don't drive it when it rains."

— Shock Wave (1996)

A 1946 Ford Club Coupe is parked between a DeSoto Adventurer and a Buick Skylark. How did this modest family-man's special find its way into Cussler's collection? Actually, he explains, it was his first acquisition.

Not long after he arrived in Denver, Cussler and his wife were driving in the country when Barbara spotted a car sitting in front of a farm with a "for sale" sign in the window. "It was like the car Barbara had in high school," Cussler says, "so we bought it. My son, Dirk, and I restored the car while it was parked in front of our house." He admits to priming it with spray cans, but "I did have the upholstery and paint done by professionals."

The modest Ford is a nice counterpoint to the glory that surrounds it. It is one of the few cars in the collection that I might be able to afford, and the spitting image of a car that a friend drove long ago. He installed a big Buick V-8 and a Hydromatic transmission in it, and, needless to say, that Ford went like a bat out of hell.

In addition to his car collection, Cussler's literary success has also provided him with the means to pursue

The 1936 Avions Voisin is one of those cars that manages to be both beautiful and ugly at the same time. Gabriel Voisin, along with Louis Bleriot, formed Europe's first commercial aircraft manufacturing company. During the pre–World War I era, many of Europe's leading aviators flew Voisin's pusher biplane. During that war Voisin continued to build aircraft, but when hostilities ceased he turned his considerable talents to building automobiles. Incorporating lightweight construction and aerodynamics, Voisin produced a series of unique vehicles between 1919 and 1939, the majority powered by Knight sleeve-valve engines. The radiator ornament on Cussler's car is an assemblage of twelve pieces of aluminum. During the 1950s, Voisin designed the Biscuter, a minicar built in Spain by Autonacional S.A.

Right: The toothy grille of the 1953 Buick Skylark. The "gun-sight" hood ornament, fins, and other applications reflected Harley Earl's appreciation for the fighter planes

his love of history. "I always liked to search for stuff," he says.

"When Dick and I owned the gas station," he continues, "we stripped down a 1948 Mercury convertible and mounted big truck tires on it—a kind of early dune buggy. We would go out into the Southern California desert and look for gold mines, ghost towns, anything we could find. Things left by early prospectors or early Spanish explorers. We never had much luck, but I think it turned me on to the challenge of the search. I have looked for shipwrecks, airplanes, steam locomotives, and people. If it's old, I'm into it."

In the late 1970s Cussler read a book by Peter Throckmorton, the dean of American marine archaeology. Throckmorton mentioned that an Englishman, Sidney Wignall, was looking for John Paul Jones's famous Revolutionary War ship, the *Bonhomme Richard*.

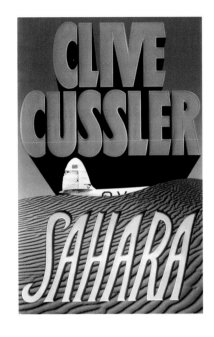

On September 23, 1779, Jones's ship had engaged the HMS *Serapis* in the North Sea off Famborough Head. The *Bonhomme Richard* lost much of its firepower and gunners in the first exchange of broadsides. Captain Richard Pearson, commander of the *Serapis*, called out to Jones, asking for his surrender, but Jones responded with his immortal reply: "I have not yet begun to fight!"

Even though their ship was sinking, *Bonhomme Richard's* marines and seamen, under Jones's direction, put up a tenacious fight. Captain Pearson finally lowered his colors, and the *Serapis* surrendered. Jones won the battle, but the *Richard*, which had been mortally wounded, sank the next day.

Cussler contacted Wignall, who said he had attempted to raise money to search for the ship but had struck out. Cussler told him that he would fund an expedition to locate the *Richard*.

As described by Cussler, that first expedition was a "comedy of errors, veering two degrees beyond a fiasco." In 1978, he chartered an old World War II British minesweeper, the *Keltic Lord*, that was loaded with "tons of unnecessary equipment" and manned by "a crew that would have made a saloon full of heavy-metal bikers hold their noses and run for the exits."

After numerous misadventures, and dropping $80,000, Cussler discovered that the wreck Wignall thought might be the *Bonhomme Richard* was actually a cargo ship sunk by a German U-boat during World War I. "In an ironic twist," Cussler says, "the *Keltic Lord*, along with its entire crew, vanished six months later without a trace in the North Sea during a winter storm."

Although the first expedition was a disaster, Cussler came back for more. "I was bitten by the bug," he says. "That next year, we didn't find the *Bonhomme Richard*, but we had a much better time of it."

Since Cussler was spending his own money, Wayne Gronquist, an attorney from Austin, Texas, suggested that he should incorporate as a nonprofit foundation. "The trustees," Cussler says, "wanted to call it the Clive Cussler Foundation, but I told them, 'No way!' I have an ego, but it isn't that big."

The organization was ultimately called the National Underwater & Marine Agency. "Now I could say, 'Yes, Virginia, there really is a NUMA,' a NUMA dedicated to preserving American marine heritage by locating and identifying lost ships of historic significance before they are gone forever."

Over the years, NUMA has found more than seventy historically significant warships, steamers, and other vessels that were thought to be lost forever. These include the *Carpathia*, the ship that rescued 706 survivors from the sinking *Titanic*; the fabled ghost ship the *Mary Celeste*; the German U-20, the submarine that sank the *Lusitania*; Sieur de La Salle's ship, *L'Aimable*, near Galveston, Texas; and the *Hunley*, the Confederate submarine.

Cussler is a fellow of the Royal Geographic Society, the American Society of Oceanographers, and the Explorers Club. The latter honored him with the Lowell Thomas Award for his underwater exploration. In 1997, the board of governors of the Maritime College, State University of New York, awarded Cussler a Doctor of Letters degree for his nonfiction book *The Sea Hunters*. It was the first time since the college was founded in 1874 that such a degree was awarded.

Considered by most to be NUMA's most important discovery, the *Hunley* was the first underwater craft to sink a warship in battle. While withdrawing, something went wrong and the Hunley went to the bottom with all hands. The legendary showman P.T. Barnum once offered $100,000 to anyone who could find the little submarine and deliver it to his museum in New York City.

Cussler first began searching for the *Hunley* in 1980, and his crew found her in May, 1995. "One morning," he says, "the phone rang about 5:00 A.M. It was Ralph

He continues, "Now, there are so many cars that we decided it's better to just leave them sit. If we have to get a car out for an event or show, we'll deal with it. Also, due to fire regulations, we cannot keep fuel or batteries in the cars. And, even if I could keep the gas tanks full, I wouldn't. Today's fuels cause problems if you leave any in the cars. After a period of time they tend to separate, and the chemicals destroy fuel lines, fuel pumps, and accelerator pumps. This creates a big problem because you can't just go out and buy parts for these cars."

Cussler is extremely particular about his vehicles. "Clive wants things a certain way," Lowden says, "and that's that. If I take off a rusty bolt, I will certainly not use it again. Clive has the means to go all the way. That makes it nice for us because we can do the best job possible."

Lowden continues, "When Clive was buying a lot of cars, we were doing frame-off restorations. Now, a lot of our work is redoing earlier restorations. Clive likes to change the color that a car is painted. I think he gets bored with them. When we change the color, it gives us a chance to go over the car and do any other work that is necessary."

As a body man he will tell you that the sanding process is probably the most important step in any restoration process. "You can do the best mechanical and body work," Lowden says, "but if you don't prepare the surface correctly, a lousy paint job will ruin the whole job."

When Lowden and Posey are getting a car ready for paint, they use a series of different sandpapers to prepare the surface. Starting with a coarse grit, each grade is less abrasive than the previous one. The final grade feels more like velvet than sandpaper. For some reason, a freshly sanded car has an almost hypnotic quality. You want to touch it, run your hand over the surface, caress it. The metal feels like a baby's bottom.

In Lowden's shop, however, you had best refrain from the urge to touch a sanded car. No matter how smooth it looks, no matter how seductive that fender or hood, do not touch.

"People come into the shop," Lowden says, scowling, "and without even thinking, they reach out and touch a car that we've spent a week sanding. It drives me crazy." He explains that everybody has oils on their fingers, and touching a sanded car will leave an oil spot on the surface. When Lowden goes to paint the car, that spot will cause what he calls a "fish eye."

A "fish eye" at Sam's Discount House o'Color may not be a disaster, but in Lowden's world it will result in having to refinish an entire body panel, if not the entire car.

Lowden is also responsible for transporting the cars to shows and events. For long distances, the cars are shipped on a closed trailer. But when a show is local, Lowden drives the car there himself. He tries to set aside at least a week to prepare a car if it is expected to run. "We have to make sure the car is cosmetically and mechanically ready to go. I've been around these cars long enough to

The glittering interior of the 1958 Oldsmobile 98. In addition to the usual options—power windows, power seats, etc.—the car had a Trans-Portable Radio that could be taken along to picnics or the beach. Stored in a locked bracket in the glove box, the radio had a stylish chrome face and operated on battery power.

know their personalities and most of the problems you can expect."

The reason for setting aside a week was made clear when we were photographing Cussler's cars for this book. A 1955 Packard Caribbean had not run for more than a year, and our attempts to push the beast into position suggested possible hernias for everyone involved.

Weighing in at a hefty 4,755 pounds, the Caribbean convertible (the model only came as a convertible) was Packard's flagship. It was added to the brand's lineup in 1953 to compete with the Cadillac Eldorado and the Buick Skylark.

Designed by Dick Teague, the flamboyant Caribbean featured a tri-tone color scheme, a glittery dashboard, tasteful chrome accents, a 275 hp V-8—fed by two four-barrel carburetors—a Twin Ultramatic transmission, and torsion-level suspension.

The Caribbean was expensive and rare. In 1955 only four hundred were built, and the car would have set its owner back $6,000.

For all their size and flash, the cars were plagued with mechanical problems. The V-8's lifters clattered, the Twin Ultramatic's seals leaked, and the suspension constantly blew fuses. The latter would leave the Caribbean squatting in an undignified stance, unbefitting its status.

Most of the problems were solved in 1956, but that was not only the last hurrah for the Caribbean, it was also the last year for "real" Packards. In 1954, Packard had merged with Studebaker. Disastrous sales in 1956 forced the company to end production of Packards. Studebaker produced a car with the Packard nameplate in 1957 and 1958, but the "Packardbakers" were not successful. A year later, Packard was no more.

Determined to get the Caribbean running, Keith climbed behind the wheel. After several minutes of fruitless cranking, he went into his shop and returned with a gas can, a can of starter fluid, jumper cables, and a fresh battery.

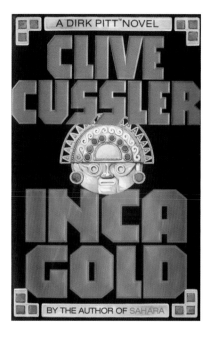

Opening the hood, he gave both carburetors a shot, and then slid into the driver's seat. The starter motor went to work again, and suddenly two fat fireballs leaped out of the carbs. We all yelled that the car was in danger of blowing up, but Keith, who kept cranking, yelled back, "That's alright, as long as I keep the starter going, it will suck the fire back down into the carbs."

Sure enough, as Lowden continued to pump the accelerator, the flames disappeared. Slowly but surely, the Packard's mighty V-8 reluctantly coughed to life.

After some additional coaxing, and a few more fireballs, Lowden had the Caribbean cruising around the parking lot. As the green-and-white beauty glided past us, Lowden looked very much at home behind the wheel.

It is obvious to me that Clive Cussler's cars are in very capable hands.

Above: Cussler's 1936 Berline is graced by this "kneeling archer" mascot. First offered as an accessory in 1928, the Rodin-inspired archer was standard equipment on most Pierce-Arrows after 1930.

Right: Clive Cussler with a pair of classic Pierce-Arrows. George Pierce opened his first business in Buffalo, New York, in 1873, manufacturing refrigerators, birdcages, iceboxes, and bathtubs. Ten years later, Pierce added bicycles to his product line and began to experiment with automobiles. The Pierce-Arrow Motor Car Co. was launched in 1907. Pierce sold his interest in the company and was replaced as president by George Birge. Pierce-Arrow was soon building luxury cars that ranked among the best in the world. President Taft, the first president to use an automobile for official occasions, ordered two Pierce-Arrows. In 1913 the company introduced its signature headlights. Molded into the front fenders, they looked like a frog's eyes. Studebaker merged with Pierce-Arrow in 1928, and a new line of cars, the Series 81, was unveiled. This was also the first year that the famous archer mascot appeared on the car. Despite the Depression, Pierce-Arrow soldiered on, introducing straight-eight and twelve-cylinder engines, but Studebaker was forced to sell the company in 1933. Despite the efforts of a group of Buffalo investors, Pierce-Arrow managed to build only a handful of cars in 1938, shortly before the company failed. Cussler's car is a 1936 Berline, powered by a V-12 flathead engine. A Berline, also called an enclosed-drive limousine, is a sedan with a partition behind the driver. The Travelodge house trailer, built in 1937, is a very rare item. Attempting to generate additional cash flow, Pierce-Arrow went into the travel-trailer business. Offered in three sizes, the trailers had an aluminum skin covering a steel frame. Hydraulic brakes were standard, and the trailers were as elegant as Pierce-Arrow's automobiles. The interior of Cussler's trailer, done in birch and gumwood, includes a dining area, ice box, gas cook stove, wood heating stove, water tank, and sleeping accommodations. In 1936 few people could afford the cars, much less the trailers, and only about 450 Travelodge trailers were produced.

Joaquin Folch

Joaquin Folch got behind his first steering wheel when he was six years old. "We have a large celebration in the Latin countries," he says. "It is called Epiphany, or Three Kings Day. On the night of the fifth of January, if you are doing well in school, the Three Kings come to your home and bring you presents, much the same as your Santa Claus." Young Joaquin must have been paying attention in class because the Three Kings brought him a go-cart. "It had a small English Villiers 75cc two-stroke engine," Folch remembers. "I drove that car for many long enjoyable hours on the gravel path in our garden."

Joaquin Folch-Rusinol i Corachan was born in Barcelona in 1953. He studied at the Deutsche Schule of Barcelona and then attended the Barcelona Institute of Technology, graduating in 1978 with a degree in industrial engineering. "In those days," he says, "I really had no idea what the future would bring for me, but one thing was very clear: I was much more comfortable with mechanical activities than, let's say, musical activity."

A year after he graduated, Folch moved to England and went to work in his brother-in-law's jewelry business for almost two years, renting a flat in London's West End. On weekends, he competed in motorcycle races. "When I was sixteen," he says, "I got my first motorcycle—also for doing well in school. Two years later, I competed in my first race, a trial in Cataluna. While I was attending the university, I was restoring Bultaco motorcycles."

Folch raced a Matchless G-50 at most of England's important circuits: Silverstone, Donington, Mallory, Snetterton, and Brands Hatch, to name a few. At the tracks, he noticed that there was a great deal of regard for the older bikes. "In England," he says, "they were very appreciated. The old Nortons, the triples, machines of that order. At the time there were a lot of bikes just like that in Spain. Some were still running, but there was very little interest in them."

Back in Spain for a visit, Folch went to see the Norton importer. "I asked him," Folch says, "if he still had any Norton John Player stuff. I was very excited when he said yes."

James Lansdowne Norton produced his first motorcycle in 1902, a bicycle powered by a Belgian Clement engine located above the front wheel. Norton Motors Ltd. went on to become one of England's premier motorcycle manufacturers, building bikes for both the road and racing. During World War II, the military took delivery of more than 100,000 Nortons.

During the early 1950s the legendary Geoff Duke rode Nortons, sponsored

by John Player cigarettes. Talented and fearless, Duke was so popular that more than 400,000 fans turned up at a German Grand Prix to watch him do battle on his Norton Manx.

Folch also went to see the Ducati importer. During the 1970s Ducati and Norton were locked in a struggle for the Spanish championship. Since each year's competition bike was faster than the previous year's model, the Norton and Ducati dealers stashed the outmoded machines in their back rooms—unwanted and unloved. Folch ended up buying them "for a pittance." Those motorcycles were the first acquisitions in a collection that now numbers more than 250.

"When I began buying motorcycles," Folch says, "I was not thinking of assembling a large collection. But, little by little, it began to grow." He grins, "I also think that collecting is a disease in our family."

Folch's grandfather, also named Joaquin, was passionate about mineralogy and geology. He traveled the world searching for mineral specimens and assembled a collection numbering more than 13,000 pieces. Recognized as a worldwide authority, he wrote numerous articles and was a member of the Barcelona Royal Academy of the Sciences and Arts. "At present," says Folch, "the minerals collection is in my home, preserved as my grandfather left it. According to the Smithsonian Institution, it is one of the best private collections in the world."

Joaquin's father, Alberto, also acquired an impressive collection, but his interests were enthnology and research into ancient cultures, in particular those at risk of disappearing forever. "While my father was in the army," Folch says, "he spent time in the Spanish territories in North Africa. That experience led him to undertake scientific expeditions to all parts of the world. My father accumulated an impressive collection of primitive art, pre-Columbian art, and Asian art. That collection is also in our home."

In 1976, Alberto set up the Folch Foundation, an organization that provides grants to museums and professional publications. In recognition of Alberto Folch's

Previous page: The courtyard at Joaquin Folch's summer home, Con Costa, provides the perfect background for Folch and his Ferrari 312 T5. The car was driven by the dashing French Canadian Giles Villeneuve during the 1980 season.

Above: Although a few years separate these two photographs of Joaquin Folch, it is apparent that he has always had an affinity for two wheels. The brand of bicycle is forgotten, but the machine displaying number eight is a 1964 Matchless G-50. This is the motorcycle that Folch raced while he was living in England.

Right: Folch's collection of motorcycles numbers more than 250. "When I began buying motorcycles," Folch says, "I was not thinking of assembling a large collection. But, little by little, it began to grow." The streamlined motorcycle against the left wall is a 175cc Bultaco that set a twenty-four-hour record in 1960 at 81.82 mph. The record still stands today.

Joaquin Folch driving a Lotus Type 49, owned and prepared by Classic Team Lotus, at the 1997 Monaco Historic Grand Prix. First raced in 1967, the Lotus 49 was the first car to be powered by the Cosworth-Ford DFV V-8 engine. This outstanding powerplant would dominate Formula 1 racing for a decade. Folch won the event, emulating Graham Hill's victories at the same course in 1968 and 1969. Folch said later, "It was my greatest victory, ever!"

Under the direction of Joaquin Folch and the company's board, planning began on a move that would provide room for future growth and bring all of the operations together for the first time. Today, Industrias Titán is located in El Prat de Llobregat, an industrial area located a short distance from the Barcelona airport, and employs 500 in its factory. During 2001 the company produced 18,000 tons of solvent-based paints and 16,000 tons of resins and emulsions, in addition to 35,000 tons of water-based paints. The company's catalogue listed more than 4,300 individual items.

When his father died, Folch found himself under a great deal of pressure from Industrias Titán's management to quit riding motorcycles. He laughs, "They did not want the boss to get killed."

He continues, "I know riding a motorcycle is dangerous, but I'm very conscious of what I'm doing. I go very gently. Also, by riding a motorcycle, I'm always on time. If you value your time, you can not use your car in Barcelona because of the traffic and parking. I even hire motorcycles in Paris, Geneva, and Zurich."

Folch's collection of motorcycles and automobiles is cloistered at his summer home, Con Costa. Located an hour's drive from Barcelona, the property, a working farm, was purchased by Folch's grandfather in 1955. "Although we are close to Barcelona," Folch says, "you feel like you are in the country. We used to keep our cars and bikes in the city, but that proved to be very inconvenient." He chuckles, "At the farm, you can start a car without somebody yelling at you."

The entrance to Con Costa is marked by an extremely discreet sign—so discreet that William and I managed to drive by several times before we found it. After we identified ourselves, two impressive gates swung open and we proceeded down a long driveway flanked by rows of plantain trees.

We were met by Jesus Gonzales and Anthony Campoy, two men who have worked for the Folch family for more than fifty years. During the 1960s, Alberto Folch was the Spanish importer for Aston Martin and Lotus, and both Gonzales and Campoy worked as mechanics. Today, they are responsible for maintaining

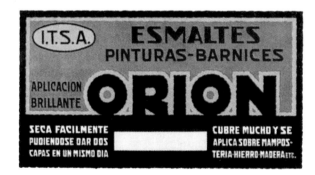

A very rare Pegaso Z-102. In 1950, engineer Wifredo Ricart decided Spain needed a car that would demonstrate to the world that the country could produce an exceptional product. It also provided Ricart with an opportunity to thumb his nose at his rival, Enzo Ferrari.

Joaquin Folch's collection and act as his crew at historic races.

We followed Gonzales across a courtyard to a pair of large doors, which he opened. On the ground floor, we found a very interesting combination of road cars and race cars lined up against both walls. The left row included a group of Aston Martins. I fell in love with Aston Martins when I saw 007 utilizing his machine guns, smoke screen, oil slick, rear bulletproof screen, and ejection seat to outwit Goldfinger's evil henchmen. Folch has six examples: a DB4GT, a DB4, a DB5, a DB6, a V8, and a Vanquish.

Later, when I was interviewing Folch, I asked him about the collection of Aston Martins. "My father drove Aston Martins because he fell in love with English cars," he says. "That's why we had the dealerships for Aston Martin and Lotus. When he saw my interest in restoring motorcycles, my father thought that I might be interested in his cars some day. All of my Aston Martins belonged to my father."

Lotus is also well represented in Folch's collection: a Type 16, a Type 23B, a Type 27, an Elan series 1, an Elan 26R, and two John Player Specials, a Type 91 and a Type 94T. The 91 and 94T are resplendent in the stylish black-and-gold livery that first appeared on a Lotus Formula 1 car in 1972.

Folch also likes Ferraris. In the garage we find a 312BB, a 364 GTB/4, a 275GTB/2, a 275GTB/4, and a 312T5. The latter car was driven during the 1980 season by Gilles Villeneuve, one of auto racing's more colorful characters.

Born in Quebec in 1950, Villeneuve started his racing career in snowmobiles, "Every winter," he commented, "you would reckon on three or four big spills—and I'm talking about being thrown onto the ice at 100 mph. Those things used to slide a lot, which taught me a great deal about control. And the visibility was terrible! Unless you were leading, you could see nothing, with all the snow blowing about. Good for the reactions—and it stopped me having any worries about racing in the rain."

Villeneuve came to the attention of Enzo Ferrari in 1977. For the next five years the Canadian's all-out driving style brought Ferrari six Grand Prix victories and made Villeneuve extremely popular with racing fans. At the 1979 French Grand Prix, Villeneuve, in a slower car, battled the Renault of René Arnoux in a wheel-banging duel, finishing 24/100s of a second ahead of the Frenchman. It was probably the most exciting second-place finish in Formula 1 history.

At Zolder in 1982, Villeneuve collided with another car

The Pegaso was named for the winged horse in Greek mythology. Only eighty-six cars had been built when production ended in 1957, but a legend had been created. There are eleven Pegasos at Con Costa: Folch's, above and left, and ten on loan to the foundation by other collectors.

slowing to enter the pits. His car cartwheeled off the track, disintegrating in the process. Although he was resuscitated at the scene, Villeneuve's injuries proved fatal and he died that evening at a local hospital. Grand Prix racing legend Niki Lauda described Villeneuve as "the perfect racing driver . . . with the best talent of all of us."

Parked in the rear of the garage we found one of the collection's crown jewels, a blood red Maserati 250F. Founded in 1914 by four brothers, Maserati built its first race car in 1926. Wilbur Shaw, driving a Maserati 8CTF, won the Indianapolis 500 in 1939, the only victory at Indy by an Italian car builder.

In the early 1950s, Maserati began work on a car for the new 2.5-liter Formula. The 250F's aluminum bodywork is elegant, with the fuel tank forming the tail of the car. The driver sits in an upright position. Stirling Moss, who drove a 250F to several victories, remarked, "It steered beautifully, and inclined toward stable oversteer, which one could exploit by balancing it against power and steering in long sustained drifts through corners."

During 1956, modifications were made to the car's body and chassis, and a year later, Juan Manuel Fangio won the World Championship driving a 250F. Fangio's win, however,

was the last hurrah for Maserati since financial problems put an end to its racing team.

Gonzales led us up a flight of stairs to the second floor, where we found motorcycles. Lots and lots of motorcycles. In addition to his Nortons and Ducatis, Folch's collection includes examples by Montesa, Bultaco, Lube, Sanglas, OSSA, Patton, Linto, AJS, Matchless, Yamaha, Honda, and, yes, even a few Harley-Davidsons.

Trying to digest what we had seen, William and I followed Gonzales down the stairs and into the main house. Every time we thought we had seen it all, he opened another door. The walls were covered with an astonishing collection of automotive posters, photographs, advertisements, and promotional material. While William was photographing one group of bikes, Gonzales gestured for me to follow him. He opened yet another door, revealing a large collection of Märklin model trains, and just beyond, a very impressive model railroad. It just kept getting better.

All too soon, it was time to join Folch for lunch. While we were eating, William commented on how nice it was to be enjoying excellent food while looking out the window

Francisco Xavier Bulto and Pedro Permanyer formed Montesa in 1944. The company first produced lightweight, rugged motorcycles that could hold up to Spain's war-torn roads. For several years, sales were good. The firm moved to a new factory, but a serious slump in the Spanish economy soon had the partners disagreeing on Montesa's future. Permanyer wanted the company to pull out of racing. Bulto, a champion racer, felt "sales follow the checkered flag." Bulto resigned and opened up his own firm, Bultaco. Fortunately, the economy improved and Bultaco was soon producing motorcycles that were both beautiful and fast. In 1965, the Metisse was introduced. Powered by a 250cc engine, the fire-breathing machine became very popular with scrambles riders. This Metisse was ridden by Spanish motocross champion Oriol Puig Bulto, Francisco Bulto's nephew. According to the chassis number, the bike is an original works' racer.

Previous spread: James Landsdowne Norton produced his first motorcycle in 1902, a bicycle powered by a one-horsepower Belgian Clement engine. Norton Motors Ltd. went on to become one of England's premier motorcycle manufacturers, building bikes for both road and track. Norton also came up with some very macho names for its motorcycles—Dominator, Atlas, and Commando.

at a Ferrari Formula 1 car parked in the sun. Joaquin and I concurred—very nice indeed.

After our meal, Folch led us to one more building that contained eleven cars. With no idea what they were, I looked at the badge on the one closest to me—a flying horse. I had read about Spain's mythical Pegaso but had never seen one. Now I was in a room with more than ten percent of the marque's production. The Pegaso represented one man's vision to convince the world that Spain could compete in the postwar sports-car marketplace, at the same time allowing him an opportunity to thumb his nose at Enzo Ferrari.

A potent red and yellow example belongs to Folch. The remainder of the Pegasos are on loan to Folch's Con Costa Foundation by other collectors. "The purpose of the foundation," Folch says, "is to raise the awareness of and to preserve the history of motorized vehicles, especially in Spain."

The combination of the civil and world wars left Spain's economy and infrastructure in ruins. Faced with a shortage of much-needed commercial vehicles, the government created the Empresa Nacional de Autocamines (ENASA). Assembly lines were erected in the old Hispano-Suiza factory in the Sequerra district of Barcelona, and, under the direction of Wifredo Ricart, ENASA began building trucks and buses.

Wifredo Ricart y Medina was born on May 15, 1897, the son of an upper-class Barcelona family. Trained as a mechanical engineer, he was also a talented artist and an accomplished pilot. By the time he was twenty-three, Ricart owned a company that designed and manufactured aircraft and automobile engines. When the Spanish Civil War broke out, Ricart and his family fled to Italy, where, in 1937, he was hired by Ugo Gobbato, the director of Alfa Romeo. Ricart was soon elevated to head of the Special Projects Section. It was while the Spaniard was working at the Alfa plant in Milan that Ricart made a lifelong enemy of Ferrari.

During the 1920s, Alfa made the decision to withdraw from racing. Ferrari, who worked for Alfa at the time, created his own company, Scuderia Ferrari, which essentially operated as Alfa Romeo's racing division. Unable to compete against the powerful machines of Auto Union and Mercedes, Alfa, a state-owned company and important symbol of Italian industry, decided that the factory would reenter racing. The company absorbed Scuderia Ferrari and brought the racing department back to Portello. Not only was Ferrari now working in the plant, he was reporting to Wifredo Ricart.

The two men took an instant dislike to each other, and Ferrari ended up leaving Alfa, with an agreement that he would refrain from racing cars under his own name for five years. This would prove of little consequence since the outbreak of World War II ended all automobile racing.

In his autobiography, Ferrari used several pages to vent his dislike for the Spanish engineer. "Ricard [Ferrari always went out of his way to spell the name incorrectly] had straight, oily hair, dressed with a sort of oriental elegance, jackets with long sleeves that didn't let me see his hands; when he held out the right one to shake, one felt an inert flesh, like that of a corpse. The Spanish friend wore enormous rubber soles, but so disproportionate that one day I wound up asking him why. With extreme seriousness, Ricard replied that it was obviously a question of the precautions that engineers take: 'The brain of a great technician, in order not to perceive the roughness of the ground and not to be subjected to irritation, must be accurately suspended.' Bothered by statements of this sort, I kept harping to Gobbato that the Spaniard undoubtedly must be an interesting personage, but for higher activities, for extremely high responsibilities, not for the design of racing cars. Gobbato criticized me severely and perhaps interpreted this judgment of mine as an expression of envy."

Associates of Ricart have stated that he was well aware of Ferrari's disdain and enjoyed pulling his leg. After Ferrari left, Ricart began work on the Tipo 162 and Tipo 512, but these programs would be brought to a grinding halt by the war.

During the war, Alfa built aircraft engines. When Ricart's contract ended in 1945, he returned to Barcelona. Under his leadership, ENASA's assembly lines were soon humming, and during the next five years the plant's production facilities were con-stantly being expanded. A diesel bus produced by ENASA was a major hit at the 1950 Paris Auto Salon.

Ferrari, who managed to survive during the war by fabricating machine tools, opened his factory in Maranello in 1944. Ferrari's 1.5-liter V-12 Type 125, the first car to bear his name, was entered in ten races during 1947, and the 166 Inter Coupe, the first Ferrari road car, was displayed at Turin in 1948.

Well aware of what Ferrari was doing, Ricart decided Spain needed a car that would eclipse those being built by his Italian rival. In 1950, work began on a no-holds-barred grand touring car called the Pegaso Z-102.

Ricart's name for his car, taken from the winged horse in Greek mythology, was a direct dig at Ferrari and his logo. "Why," he would ask,

CHAMPIONNAT DU MONDE DES CONDUCTEURS
XVIII E GRAND PRIX
MONACO
29 MAI 196
SELLES
LAMPLU
BREITLING

Robs Lamplough

During the early nineteenth century, a structure that would become known as the Forge Barn was erected on the 30,000-acre Oxfordshire estate of Lord Wantage. Measuring sixty feet long by thirty-five feet wide, with a cathedral ceiling almost thirty feet high, the sturdy building housed a sawmill and a blacksmith's forge. For more than a century, the estate's smiths labored at their anvils, producing the horseshoes, hardware, wagon wheels, weapons, and tools necessary for the lord's vast agricultural empire. The Industrial Revolution made it cheaper to mass-produce items than to fabricate them in the farm's shop. At the beginning of the twentieth century, the forge was dismantled and the sawmill moved to a new brick building; and, in the years between the World Wars, the Forge Barn was relegated to the storage of hay, straw, and food for the pigs.

By the 1970s, the managers of the estate, feeling that the Forge Barn had outlived its usefulness, wanted to tear it down and develop the property. The building, however, was on the list of Great Britain's Buildings of Historical Interest. The preservation community wanted to save the building but, as is often the case, there were no funds available to purchase the barn, much less move it and restore it. The two factions soon found themselves at an impasse.

Robs Lamplough, the owner of Manor Farm, located in the neighboring county of Berkshire, happened to hear of the Forge Barn's plight. "Ten years ago," Lamplough says, "I went over to Oxfordshire to see another historic structure that was in the process of being torn down. I asked a workman if there was another building that might be available, and he told me about the Forge Barn."

Lamplough went to see the barn, realized its potential, and quickly offered to buy it. His plan was to dismantle the structure and have it shipped to his farm, where it would be rebuilt.

A few weeks later, carpenters began to remove the shiplap siding. Once that was accomplished, they drove the oak pegs out of the barn's massive beams, using the original drift that had been discovered when the barn was cleaned out. The carpenters also discovered Roman numerals chiseled into the beams by the original builders. These proved extremely useful when it came time for reassembly. Once the structure was dismantled, it was loaded on trucks for the thirty-mile trip

Previous page: In 1994, Robs Lamplough purchased the Forge Barn, a structure dating from the early 1800s. He had it moved to his estate, Manor Farm, where it was rebuilt and renovated. Today, the Forge Barn serves as Manor Farm's office, and a combination family room and entertainment hall. The building is also home to Lamplough's library and collection of aviation and auto-racing memorabilia.

Above: Lamplough driving for a paycheck at England's Silverstone track in 1971. The "Lamplola," a hybrid car built by Lamplough, combined Lola F2 and F5000 components.

Right: It must be England. The distinctive elliptical front wing, known to racing fans as the "tea tray," identifies this car as a March 711. In 1971, Ronnie Peterson, the "Super Swede," finished runner-up to Jackie Stewart in the World Championship driving a 711.

to Manor Farm. The first order of business was sandblasting two hundred years of soot and grime from the timbers and rafters. Rotten sections were patched with wood dating from the early nineteenth century. The bricks used to build the original foundation were also recovered and used in the reconstruction.

Work on the "new" building began in early summer 1994, and the framing was completed by fall. During the winter, the unfinished structure was left exposed to the elements to allow the wood to achieve an overall patina. When the weather improved, the roof tiles were installed, along with the original siding.

Today, the Forge Barn serves as Lamplough's office and library, as well as a family room and entertainment hall. The interior is filled with Robs's collections of aviation and auto-racing memorabilia, as well as artifacts saved from old churches, pubs, country houses, and railway stations that have been demolished.

An immense fireplace, equipped with the barn's original forge bellows, is located in the center of the room, and an ornate Victorian iron chandelier illuminates an antique billiard table. Cast-iron railings embellish two balconies

connected by an overhead gallery. The stair treads are made of decorative grilles rescued from a razed Victorian church's heating system.

It was not simply a whim that convinced Lamplough to save the Forge Barn. "I've always been fascinated by history and mechanical excellence," he states. "As far back as I can remember, I have been interested in machinery. How it works, why it works, what it does. I think that is the thread that runs throughout my collections, and why I went into motor racing and became involved with airplanes."

Lamplough's grandfather worked at the Royal Aircraft Factory at Farnborough. Founded in 1908 as His Royal Majesty's Balloon Factory, the factory was responsible for a number of memorable aircraft, including the SE5 and DH4, two of the best Allied planes of World War I. Today, Farnborough is the Aerospace Division of Great Britain's Defence Research Agency.

Lamplough's grandfather was responsible for several inventions, including the Lamplough Dart, a weapon used to attack the German zeppelins (named after Count Zeppelin) that bombed London during World War I. Carried aloft by an

Above: Robs Lamplough began his racing career in 1962, driving a Mini Cooper saloon in amateur events. Two years later, he turned professional and competed in Formula Junior, Formula 5000, Formula 3, Formula 2, and Formula 1. Lamplough retired from professional racing in 1971, but is still active in historic racing.

Left: A collection of Formula cars that Lamplough drives in historic events. The car on the left, a Lotus Type 64 Indianapolis car, almost ended up buried in a hole. Based on the four-wheel-drive, turbine-powered Lotus Type 56, sponsored by Andy Granatelli and STP and raced at Indy in 1968, the Type 64 was powered by turbocharged, double-overhead-camshaft Ford V-8 engines producing anywhere between 700 and 1,000 horsepower. The cars were withdrawn from the race because of defective rear wheel hubs. After negotiations broke down between Colin Chapman and Granatelli, Chapman uttered his now famous proclamation: "Bring the cars back to Hethel. I will personally put a hacksaw through them, I will personally dig a hole, and I will personally bury them." Luckily, Chapman never made good on his threat.

airplane, the three-foot-square collapsible dart was dropped over the zeppelin, which flew at altitudes as high as 20,000 feet. If the pilot's aim was true, the dart would tear through the airship's cloth-covered hydrogen-filled cells, hopefully bringing the marauder down. The darts were superseded by incendiary bullets, which brought a flaming end to the German giants.

Lamplough was born in Gloucestershire and spent his childhood in western England. "I was born on June 4, 1940, the day of the Dunkirk evacuation." He jokes, "I arrived on England's darkest day." His father, a civil engineer, enlisted in the Royal Air Force on the day England declared war on Germany. He was initially assigned to an auxiliary unit in Oxford, but was then shipped to Rhodesia (now Zimbabwe) and trained to become a fighter pilot. "By the time my father finished training," Lamplough says, "the Battle of Britian was over. He was sent to Africa for ferrying duties, flying Hurricanes, Spitfires, and P40 Kitty Hawks."

When the war ended, John Lamplough decided to remain in the RAF. There were more than nine hundred air bases in the United Kingdom, and the government, facing a bleak postwar economy, began to shut them down. "When a base would close," Lamplough says, "my father would be reassigned. We'd pick up and move." He chuckles, "I went to nine different schools in a thirteen-month period."

Realizing that this nomadic state of affairs could have a negative effect on their son's education, Lamplough's parents sent him to Westcliff, a boarding school. After graduating from Westcliff in 1958, Lamplough was awarded a scholarship and enrolled at Cranwell, the Royal Air Force Academy. Opened on February 5, 1920, Cranwell was the world's first military air academy. Lamplough says, "Looking back, I was like any young school boy growing up in the 1950s. Without

a clear idea of what I wanted to do, I naturally gravitated to what I grew up with. We always lived on airbases, surrounded by airplanes and pilots, and there were always flying suits and helmets hanging on hooks in our house."

Lamplough's father's rank also provided his son with a unique opportunity. "On several bases," he says, "my father was the head instructor. Flying was under his direct control. All British schoolboys were considered Air Cadets, so all I had to do was don my uniform and present myself on the flight line. If there were any spare rides, I got to go up."

Lamplough had completed two years at Cranwell when his father was killed in a flying accident. "He and another instructor," Lamplough says, "went up for a joyride in a De Havilland Chipmunk, the RAF elementary trainer. They simply spun into the ground."

After his father's death, Lamplough dropped out of Cranwell. "I stopped flying because I thought it was too dangerous," he says. "Flying had killed my father. Then, since I had to do something else, I went immediately into car racing." He smiles, "That shows how logically I was thinking at the time."

Lamplough began his racing career in 1962, driving a Mini Cooper saloon in amateur events. "In those days," he says, "it was a lot easier to become involved with racing. You got yourself a car, stuck some numbers on the side, and turned up at the racetracks."

After racing a Lotus 23 in 1963 and a Lotus 20 Formula Junior in 1964, Lamplough made the decision to turn professional. "I bought a Brabham BT8 from Bill Knight in the summer of 1964, and raced it at one event at Goodwood," he says. "The car was then shipped to Canada." Lamplough raced in the Canadian

Above: This extremely rare Lancia Stratos was the first production vehicle built specifically as a rally car. Produced from 1973 to 1978, the Stratos was fitted with fiberglass bodywork and powered by a Ferrari 246 Dino V-6. During the late 1970s and early 1980s, the car brought three World Rally Championships to Lancia.

Right: If Lampough has a favorite car, it is the BRM P133. "It's been through so much with me," he says. "I've had the car for nearly thirty-five years. I drove it during my professional career and, later, in vintage racing. The records indicate that Pedro Rodriguez and myself are the only two drivers who have raced the car."

Grand Prix at Mosport Park in September, and then headed south to California, competing in the Los Angeles Times Grand Prix at Riverside and the Pacific Grand Prix at Laguna Seca.

His last event in 1964 was the Nassau Speed Week. Held between 1954 and 1966 in the Bahamas, the Speed Weeks were not championship races but a series of independent events that gave the drivers an opportunity to enjoy spirited competition as well as some end-of-season fun in the sun.

In these days of blatant corporate sponsorship—when a race car is a rolling billboard and winning drivers are international superstars—it is hard to imagine the environment Lamplough was competing in. "Nobody had a sponsor in those days," he says. "You were not allowed to advertise on your car in Europe. I'd ring up a race promoter and say, 'Hi, I'm Robs Lamplough, I've got this car and I want to come to your race meeting. How much are you going to pay me to come?' Things were so tight that I couldn't afford a full-time mechanic. I would have to pick somebody up as I went along."

A promoter, needing to field enough cars to make up a race, would offer a driver in Lamplough's bracket travel and lodging money, pay him start money, and, if he did well, award him prize money. "Manufacturers would also provide me with anything that was consumable," he says. "Oil, fuel, spark plugs, brake pads, and tires. British Petroleum also paid for shipping the car."

Lamplough raced against the best. "I remember them all," he says. "Jim Clark, Graham Hill, Emerson Fittipaldi, Dan Gurney, A. J. Foyt, Jackie Stewart, and Jochen Rindt." He grimaces, "Each weekend I lined up with them on the grid, waiting for the start. You didn't go to race-car-driving school. You learned it on the track. I'd grit my teeth and wait for Jimmy Clark, thinking, 'Robs, maybe you can hang in with him for two corners, hopefully three, maybe even four,' and then, I'd probably spin off."

He picks up a framed photograph on his desk and hands it to me. A younger Lamplough, wearing a white racing suit, regards the camera with a self-assured look, as a mechanic makes some last-minute adjustments to his car. "I think I was

what you would call a fall guy," he says. "If Jim Clark or Jackie Stewart were going to be world champion, they needed somebody to race against. A promoter had to pad the field."

I pointed out to Lamplough that he was doing himself a serious injustice. Anybody who has raced at Lamplough's level, competing against some of the world's finest drivers, obviously knows his way around a racetrack.

He shrugs, "Well, maybe, but I have always tried to take a realistic view of anything I do. At the end of the day you see where you slot into the whole thing. In all fairness to myself, I probably slotted somewhere in the middle. The best drivers were driving a factory car with a bit more powerful engine than I had. They had three full-time mechanics and I had a guy I picked up at the track. I was also up at two o'clock in the morning, working on my car, while the other drivers, who were supposedly in bed, were probably having a party in a nightclub."

During 1965, Lamplough drove the Brabham and Lotus, competing in the Formula 3 European Championship series. He purchased a Lola in 1966 and spent the next three years racing in Formula 2. In 1969 and 1970, he drove a Lotus 43 in Formula 5000.

Introduced in Britain in 1968, Formula 5000 featured cars powered by American V-8s. The cars were fast but less sophisticated, and therefore, less expensive, than Formula 1 racers. The sport of racing was in the doldrums, and it was hoped that the new formula would bring back the crowds. Proving to be extremely popular with racing fans, the Formula 5000 series ran until 1976 and featured some of racing's most important manufacturers and drivers.

When Lamplough realized that his performance on the track was not going to make him wealthy, he went into the race-car parts business. "I had to find another angle. That was the 1960s," he says. "Great Britain was the major supplier of equipment for true racing. It still is, for that matter. All of the Indy cars are made here in England. I took advantage of the contacts I had made racing: Colin Chapman of Lotus, Eric Broadley of Lola, John Cooper, and so on. I became an exporter, selling complete cars and parts, engines, gearboxes, suspension parts,

Above: The Forge Barn's interior is filled with artifacts, including this graceful wall clock. The majority of the items were saved from old churches, pubs, country houses, and railway stations that were being demolished.

Right: Manor Farm from the cockpit of Lamplough's Gazelle helicopter, with William and myself aboard. The nave and transept of All Saints Church, in the foreground, date from Norman times. An impressive stained-glass window, installed in 1684, depicts God surrounded by forty-four saints.

radiators—any component that was in a race car. The business was headquartered in London and was very successful."

Lamplough's last professional ride was a BRM V12 that he raced in Formula I during the 1970 and 1971 seasons. In 1971, Lamplough made the decision to retire from professional racing and bought, of all things, an airplane. His experiences on the track must have convinced him that flying was not as dangerous as he thought.

"I bought a Harvard," he says. "It was an airplane that I was familiar with because I flew them while I was at Cranwell." Produced during World War II by North American, the Harvard is the British equivalent of the famous AT-6 Texan. The two-place trainer is powered by a 600-horsepower Pratt & Whitney engine and has a top speed of 210 mph. "The next thing I knew," he says, "a local policeman rang me up and asked me if I would put on a flying display for his unit's reunion. I had never done that kind of flying before, so I went out and practiced a few loops and rolls. That's how I got into display flying. You certainly couldn't do that today."

Lamplough was by then living in the Kensington section of London and working in real estate, a business that he is still involved in today. He met his wife, Widge, while he was racing, and they were married in 1976. "She

was the sister of a Formula 2 competitor," he says, laughing. "I wasn't pinching anyone's girlfriend, I just pinched someone's sister."

Once Lamplough mastered aerobatics in the Harvard, he began to look around for something faster. In 1976, he made the decision to acquire a World War II war bird. There was only one problem. His real-estate business was good, but not that good. "At that time," he says, "a flying Spitfire was going for 30,000 pounds sterling. Today it sounds ridiculous, but then that was a lot of money."

Lamplough had heard rumors that there were abandoned World War II fighter planes in Israel. "I ended up going over there," he says, "and dragging back a Hurricane, four Spitfires, and eight P-51 Mustangs."

During the late 1940s, jet fighters began to replace the piston-powered aircraft of World War II. The United States and England sold their unwanted Mustangs, Thunderbolts, Spitfires, Hurricanes, and Sea Furys to nations that could not afford the new technology. When these countries were able to enter the jet age, the once-proud fighters were scrapped or abandoned.

Lamplough gives credit to Ed Jurist, the dean of war bird collectors, for his inspiration. Jurist, who owned the Vintage Car Store in Nyack, New York, was an 8th Air Force combat veteran. Like Lamplough, Jurist was as enthusiastic about airplanes as he was about cars. He is credited with salvaging more World War II fighter planes than any other nonmilitary individual.

"Ed preceded me," Lamplough says. "It was hearing about what he did that convinced me I could do the same thing. The only difference was that he went to Peru and I went to the Middle East. Every kid in Israel has to learn about war, so why not give them a tank or fighter plane to play on instead of a swing set or sand box? When the Israeli Air Force transitioned to jets, they would give a P-51 to a kibbutz and put it in the playground so the kids could climb on it. The kids, of course, tore them up. When the toy gets busted, it gets chucked in the corner. That's when I appeared on the scene."

The airplanes that Lamplough found could best be described as hulks. The Plexiglas canopies had been destroyed, and the cockpits were trashed from exposure to the weather. The instruments and seats were long gone, and the controls were missing. "But," Lamplough says, "the engines were there, the propellers were there, the landing gear was there. Those are the components that made the airplanes so desirable."

During his quest, Lamplough was not traveling first class. "I was staying in one-star or below hotels," he says, " and eating, what you call in America, the blue-plate special." Lamplough was so short of funds that he had to rent a camel instead of a car. The dromedaries ultimately proved to be an advantage: it was easy to spot the abandoned airplanes from his vantage point on the animal's hump.

After he located the airplanes, Lamplough had them shipped back to the Imperial War Museum at Duxford. "It cost a few thousand each to send them back," he says. "They were certainly worth more than that."

The War Museum's directors provided Lamplough with free workspace, and a dedicated group of enthusiasts donated their time to help with the P-51D and Spitfire restorations. "Part of the deal," Lamplough says, "was that the airplanes would be on display while the work was going on."

He continues, "It's a curious thing. You see a beautifully done-up airplane or car, either in a museum or at an airport or track. Once you've looked it over, you've pretty well seen all there is. It's far more interesting to see a machine with

the outer skin off and people working on it." Using pieces from the eight P-51s and four Spitfires, he and the Duxford volunteers were able to produce one flying example of each plane. The restoration of each plane took ten years.

Two of the greatest airplanes of all time, the North American P-51 Mustang and the Supermarine Spitfire are assured a place in any fighter hall of fame for their outstanding performance and functional beauty. The exploits of the pilots who flew them in combat have become legends.

The Spitfire was first off the ground. In 1930, the British Air Ministry put out bids for a day-and-night fighter equipped with four guns. Reginald Mitchell, the man responsible for the famous Supermarine racing seaplanes, designed a gull-winged monoplane. When it failed to pass the Air Ministry's requirements, Mitchell went back to his drawing board.

The Air Ministry had raised the ante, now requiring eight guns. Not wanting to use a thicker wing—which would increase drag—Mitchell utilized the graceful elliptical wing, the Spitfire's most characteristic feature. On March 5, 1936, his Type 37/34 made its maiden flight, and two months later test pilot Jeffrey Quill achieved 348 mph at 17,000 feet.

On June 11, 1937, Mitchell died after a long battle with cancer, having only seen the prototype fly. His assistant, Joseph Smith, shared Mitchell's passion for the project and took over the Supermarine design office. It would be Smith who would design the forty future Spitfire variants.

When it came time to name the airplane, Sir Robert McClean, the chairman of Vickers Aviation Ltd., decided it should suggest something venomous, beginning with an "S." Although Shrike and Shrew were among the proposed monikers, Spitfire won out.

On October 16, 1939, the Spitfire had an auspicious debut. A group of German Junkers Ju 88 bombers attacked British warships in the Firth of Forth. Nine of the Ju 88s were intercepted by three Spitfires of the 603 Squadron, and one of the enemy aircraft was hit repeatedly before crashing into the sea. Other Spitfires from the 603 and 602 Squadrons shot down one more Ju 88 and two Heinkel He 111s.

The Spitfire served throughout the entire war, being constantly altered to meet changing demands. The elegant fighter was utilized as a low- and high-altitude fighter, modified to operate off aircraft carriers, and used for photoreconnaissance. A total of 20,334 Spitfires had been assembled by the time production ended in 1947.

Like the Spitfire, the P-51 was originally developed for the British. In 1939 the Royal Air Force, realizing that war was imminent, was desperate for fighters. North American Aviation's Lee Atwood and Edgar Schmued conceived the NA-73, and a prototype flew for the first time on October 26, 1940. Assigned the XP-51 designation, the airplane was one of the first fighters to use a laminar-flow airfoil, a feature that became standard on most later high-performance fighters.

Produced jointly by Britain and France during the 1970s, the Gazelle served with all four branches of the British armed forces and is still one of the fastest helicopters ever built. When the RAF retired a number of the aircraft, Lamplough bought twelve. He maintains four in flying condition and uses the others for parts.

Although originally called the Apache, the airplane soon became known as the Mustang. To improve high-altitude performance, the P-51's Allison engines were replaced with Rolls-Royce Merlins. The 1,695-horsepower engine gave the P-51D a top speed of 437 mph at 25,000 feet. Pilots flying Mustangs in Europe destroyed 4,950 enemy aircraft. A total of 14,819 Mustangs were built for the U.S. Army. They were used as dive-bombers, bomber escorts, and interceptors, and for strafing and photoreconnaissance.

When the war ended, P-51s and Spitfires continued to be used by the U.S. Air Force and the RAF. Mustangs flew combat missions in Korea, and the last offensive sorties flown by RAF Spitfires took place on January 1, 1951, in China.

Now that he had not one, but two war birds, Lamplough began to use them for exhibition flying. "During the 1980s," he says, "there was a great deal of interest in those airplanes. A war bird is a very fast airplane, and I can fly from here to Paris in under an hour. If I timed it right, there were occasions when I could do three, even four shows in a weekend." Lamplough has also performed with his aircraft in several films. When Ben Affleck took on the Luftwaffe in the opening scenes of *Pearl Harbor*, Lamplough was flying one of the Spitfires. He also flew his P-51 in the Bruce Willis film *Hart's War*.

One of his most recent film projects was *Dark Blue World*, a film documenting the exploits of several Czechoslovakian pilots who volunteered to fly with the RAF during World War II. In it, Lamplough and fellow pilot Nigel Lamb fly Spitfires. "We spent five weeks at an abandoned Russian airbase," Lamplough says. "It was a wild place to film, but quite enjoyable. Flying an antique fighter in a film presents some unique problems."

He uses his hands to demonstrate: "Squeezing two planes in formation among trees and hills is a risky business. Also, wearing the costumes—the flying jacket, the Mae West lifejacket, a helmet, and goggles—makes it authentic, but not so easy for us." He laughs, "The chaps flying in the war were in their early

The Bucker Bu 133 Jungmeister (Young Master) flew for the first time in 1935. Designed for the Luftwaffe as an advanced aerobatic trainer, the airplane pushed the limits of the restraints placed on German aviation in the Versailles Treaty. The Jungmeister has a maximum speed of 135 mph.

for auction. Lamplough bought twelve. He maintains four in flying condition and uses the others for parts.

We end our expedition at the hangar. Inside we find two of the aforementioned helicopters, a Yak C.18a, a Beechcraft Staggerwing, a Bucker Jungmeister, and a Fokker Dr.1 reproduction. The remainder of Lamplough's aircraft are kept at North Weald Aerodome in Essex.

By now, the weather has improved, and Lamplough suggests we might like to see Manor Farm from the air. William and I make our way to an olive-drab Gazelle where Adrian Ayres, Lamplough's mechanical engineer, is finishing preflight inspection. A few minutes later, Lamplough climbs into the pilot's seat. He gives us a quick familiarization and hits the starter. The turbine comes to life.

A few minutes later we are circling the area. Rolling hills, flocks of sheep, stately manor houses tucked into trees—it is like something out of *National Geographic*. Lamplough explains that he has to avoid certain fields because there is a bird hunt planned for the next day and he would not want to spook the intended prey. I wonder how the birds react when he shows up in his Spitfire.

All too soon we turn back to Manor Farm, and a few minutes later we are on the ground. On the way back to his office, Lamplough says, almost gleefully, "I got my helicopter license six weeks ago." William and I look at each other. After a brief moment of distress, I remember a quote attributed to Baron Manfred von Richthofen, also known as the Red Baron: "The quality of the box matters little. Success depends on the man who sits in it."

Above: Lamplough has flown his Spitfire in several films, including *Pearl Harbor* and *Dark Blue World*. The latter, filmed at an abandoned Soviet base north of Prague, tells the story of two Czechoslovakian pilots who flew with the RAF during World War II. It required three days to add the "makeup"—oil, exhaust, gunport stains, scratches, and the correct squadron markings—to Lamplough's Spitfire so it would look like a combat veteran.

Right: Lamplough in the cockpit of *Miss Helen*. Arriving in Europe early in 1945, the P-51D was assigned to Captain Raymond H. Littge as his personal aircraft. Littge named the airplane after his girlfriend, Helen Fisher, whom he married after the war. Littge, an ace, had ten-and-a-half confirmed kills. After the war, the airplane was exported to Sweden and then sold to Israel, where it ended up as a piece of playground equipment at Ein Gedi Kibbutz. Rescued from oblivion, *Miss Helen* is flown by Lamplough in air shows and films.

Harry Mathews

The sun was beginning to heat things up when we arrived at the Pueblo Motorsports Park. I had driven down to the southern Colorado city with Harry Mathews, his son, Greg, and his son-in-law, Mark Burgard. They were going to work the kinks out of their three McLarens before heading off to compete in a Can-Am (Canadian-American Challenge Cup) event at Road America in Elkhart Lake, Wisconsin. The track, operated by the city of Pueblo, is located on the town's outskirts and combines a road course with a drag strip. Mathews's car carrier had arrived earlier, and the three McLarens were already being fussed over by George Widich and Greg Jacobs, the mechanical wizards who keep the Mathews stable running. The only other vehicles on the track were a shrieking, flashy motorcycle and a functional-looking, rather trucklike machine tuning up for the upcoming Pike's Peak hill climb. The temperature was hovering around ninety, and the Mathews team broke into a sweat as they donned their racing gear and slid into the McLarens.

T he engines came to life with an ear-shattering bellow. Pulling out onto the track in formation—Harry in the M6A, Greg in the M8F, and Mark in the M1C—the three McLarens disappeared in a howling cloud of savagery. If three of these beasts make this much noise, what was it like when thirty-plus shared the track in the glory days of Can-Am racing?

The motorcycle rider parked his crotch rocket, ambled over, and asked me how long the "guys" were going to be out on the track. I explained that I really did not know what was going on, but my understanding was that they were doing a little tuning. Obviously intimidated by the sound and fury, he and his cohorts loaded the bike on their truck and departed.

When the Mathews squadron pulled off the track, Greg casually remarked to Widich that he did not have any brakes. After a brief discussion, they decided that the high temperature was causing the brake fluid to boil.

While they were working on the car, Harry handed me a helmet. "What's this for?"

"You wanted a ride," he said, pointing to the car. Yes, in a moment of bravado I had suggested I might like to go for a ride, but that was then. This was now.

With no easy way out, I was given a quick course on what not to lean on when getting into a race car. It was immediately apparent that these cars were designed for lean men of speed, not middle-aged writers. After some hasty refitting by Jacobs, I managed to squeeze my butt into the seat and, sucking it in, to buckle the seat and shoulder belts.

Once I put the helmet on, it really began to get hot. The mechanics were still making adjustments to the brakes and—just as a wave of claustrophobia began to threaten to overwhelm me—Greg reached out a gloved hand and the engine snarled to life.

Jacobs gave us a thumb's up, and soon we were going very fast, or so I thought. I did not know it, but Greg was letting the engine warm up before he got on it. Suddenly, as we began a sweeping turn that led to the track's main straightaway, all hell broke loose.

The sound of the 850-horsepower Chevrolet was almost unbearable, and each shift produced a slight pause, followed by the feeling that I was being

Previous spread: Harry Mathews's collection lined up at his Arvada, Colorado, business headquarters. Mathews considers his world-class collection of McLarens to be his crown jewels. "In 1961," he says, "I saw Bruce McLaren and Denny Hulme race at Road America. At the time I never dreamed I would have the honor to keep their legacy and incredible racing history alive."

Left: Harry Mathews with his 1955 Plymouth sometime in the late 1950s. "I don't remember much about that car," Mathews says. "I went through a lot of cars in those days."

Above: Harry and Greg Mathews photographed in the showroom where the majority of the car collection is displayed. In addition to Mathews's signature McLarens, the collection features a wide assortment of sports cars, single-seat Formula cars, hot rods, motorcycles, and special-interest cars.

With everybody running, we pulled out. After a few missed shifts that Mark did his best to ignore, I had the car somwhat under control as we began our spirited descent down Route 70 from the mountains. Harry, in a Ferrari, was out in front; I was second. In the Cobra's dainty rear-view mirror, I could see the rest of the cars strung out behind us.

A truck boxed Harry in, and, as I pulled out to pass, a kid in a pickup truck leaned out and yelled, "Is it a real one?" Startled, I nodded yes, and, as the lane opened up in front of me, I stuck my foot in it.

The car's rear end shimmied a little bit, and then the Cobra got up and went. By now I was well aware of the flaws that Harry had enumerated. The seat is not very comfortable, the steering wheel is at an awkward angle, there is not adequate room for your legs and feet, it is extremely hot, even when you are going fast, and the noise is horrendous. But, at that point, I really did not care. The view over those macho fenders when you are going like a bat out of hell is like nothing else I've experienced.

As the speedometer rolled past 100, I backed off. The rest of the drive was uneventful, except for the car's tendency to overheat in traffic and the constant attention the car attracts. Several drivers almost ran into us, they were so busy gawking. That kind of attention can be very disconcerting, although I'm sure I could get used to it.

I pulled into Mathews's lot, grateful to get the Cobra back in one piece. Greg walked over and asked me what I thought about the car. I told him it was fantastic. Harry heard me. "That car," he corrected, "is a dinosaur." Greg shrugged, looked down at those wonderful fenders, and added, "But dad, it's a classic dinosaur."

All business. The velocity stacks on the McLaren M8F's Chevrolet engine are designed to get as much air as possible into the cylinders. Putting out a healthy 800 horsepower, the big-block Chevys ruled Can-Am racing until Porsche arrived with its mighty Panzers.

If you are a mechanic and want to work at Mitchell Motors Ltd., you'd better be good. On a recent visit to the shop, located in Littleton, a suburb south of Denver, there was an immaculate MG TC in for a tune up, a Ferrari waiting for a turbocharger and digital fuel injection, a stately 1928 Rolls-Royce Phantom I undergoing a frame-off restoration, a Hummer halfway through a 454 Vortec engine swap—described by shop owner, Roger Mitchell, as "trying to put ten pounds in a five pound sack"—a 1953 Chevrolet, still driven by its original owner, undergoing a brake job, and Mitchell's own project car, a 1938 Ford coupe powered by a supercharged Rolls-Royce engine. The first thing you notice about the nearly 19,000-square-foot facility is how clean it is. This is not a "Gasoline Alley" operation with oil spots on the floor and greasy denizens swinging wrenches. Roger Mitchell believes it is essential for the kind of business he runs to have an immaculate shop.

M y customers expect it," he says. "The two best investments I ever made are my pop machine—so I don't have to pay for them—and my floor scrubber."

Roger Mitchell's destiny was sealed on his twelfth birthday. "My parents," he recalls, "gave me a box of tools and an automobile engine. It was a Ford, and the tool box had a bunch of hand wrenches and sockets." He laughs, "I never did get the engine to run, but I certainly found out what was inside."

His enthusiasm for things mechanical led Mitchell to a series of experiments with the family lawnmower. "My dad and I had a running battle," he says. "I was always taking the muffler off and bolting on different styles of exhaust pipes. I also messed around with the fuel, anything to make the lawnmower faster and louder. My father was not amused because he thought a lawnmower was a machine designed for mowing the lawn, not a race car with blades."

Mitchell next tried to convince his parents that he needed a motor scooter and, like most parents, they were not fond of the idea. "I kept after them," he says,

Previous page: Three American hot dogs: Roger Mitchell, Indy car connoisseur; the Coney Island hot dog stand, a Colorado landmark; and a 1994 Penske PC-23 (the PC stands for Penske Car). Driven by Emerson Fittipaldi in the 1994 Indianapolis 500, the Mercedes push-rod-engine-powered car was leading until Fittipaldi crashed, late in the race. Driving a duplicate Penske, Al Unser Jr. took the checkered flag.

Above: Roger Mitchell's first Indy car was a 1979 PC-7. He purchased the car in 1985 and has driven it often in vintage races. Mitchell is a major fan of Indy-type racing. "I've always wanted to be around Indy cars," he says. "I've even had the opportunity to work in the pits for several teams at Indy."

Right: Wearing number twenty-five, a 1987 PC-16 that Rick Mears drove in the 1987 Indianapolis 500 and CART. "I'm a big Rick Mears fan," Mitchell says of the four-time Indy winner.

"and finally my dad told me I could have one if I paid for it. I think he figured I'd never be able to come up with the money."

After toiling at a series of odd jobs, and a lot of looking, Mitchell managed to find a basket case that fit his budget. "It was an old Cushman," he says, "in 13 million pieces."

When, after a year's labor in the basement, it began to look like Roger might actually get the scooter to run, Mitchell's parents told him he could attend driving school and get his driver's license. There was, however, one stipulation.

"I had to get rid of the scooter," he says. "Looking back, it was probably one of the best things my mom and dad did for me because I probably would have killed myself on that thing." Mitchell was working in a gas station after school and on weekends, and, a few weeks after he got his license, he bought a used 1958 Chevrolet.

Mitchell was born in Columbia, South Carolina. While he was growing up, his family moved around a lot. "When I was very young my father worked in construction, and we spent three and a half years in North Africa. When we got back to the United States, we lived in South Carolina. While we were there, my father did a little bit of dirt racing with a couple of his buddies."

During the 1950s, Mitchell's father drove a truck for Navajo Freight Lines. He then sold parts for Mack Trucks, before going to work for the White Motor Company. In 1968, when Roger was a junior in high school, his father was transferred to Springfield, Missouri.

"I finished high school in Springfield," he says, "and then enlisted in the Navy. I was badly injured in a fall, and, after I was discharged, I went to Southwest Missouri State in Springfield."

After one year, Mitchell moved to St. Louis and enrolled at Washington University. "General Motors was paying my tuition," he says. "In return, I worked on the Chevrolet assembly line."

Mitchell was a "Ten-Man." This meant he could handle ten other jobs on the assembly line as well as his own. I can appreciate the importance of Mitchell's assignment, having spent some time myself on the line in a Chevrolet engine plant. You never left your job when the line was running. If you needed to go to the restroom, you put up your hand and tried to get the attention of a Ten-Man. He would take over your job until you got back. It was extremely important to be on good terms with the Ten-Man.

In 1971 Mitchell was laid off, and a year later he moved to Denver. "I got a job with Kenz & Leslie, a company that built race cars. I worked there for two years, doing engine work in the shop."

Bill Kenz and Roy Leslie began their racing careers driving midget oval-track cars in the 1930s. In the 1950s, they built "777," a streamliner that was the first car of its kind to exceed 200 mph at the Bonneville salt-flats. The racing duo went on to build a series of very successful dragsters and funny cars.

A 1989 PC-18 (front) and a 1990 PC-16. The PC-18 carries serial number one and was driven by Rick Mears in the 1989 Indianapolis 500. Mears sat on the pole and ended up finishing twenty-third. Mitchell is an unqualified fan of Roger Penske. "Mr. Penske is one of the finest men in racing," Mitchell says. "He and his people just seem to know how to do things better."

Top: A 1986 March. Driven by Emerson Fittipaldi during the 1986 and 1987 seasons, this car had the best record of any March car that ever participated in CART.

Bottom: A 1988 PC-17 driven by Danny Sullivan in the 1988 Indianapolis 500. Sullivan, after leading the race for ninety-one laps, clipped the wall twice on lap 102 and ground to a halt. That same year, Sullivan won the CART PPG Championship Cup in this car.

Leaving Kenz & Leslie, Mitchell went to work for Kumpf Lincoln and Mercury to perform warranty work on Panteras. "I enjoyed working on Panteras," he says. "You hear all sorts of horror stories about them, but it's like any kind of car, you just have to know how they work."

In the late 1960s Henry Ford III wanted to build a car to compete with the Corvette. Since he already had an Italian wife, he tried unsuccessfully to buy several Italian car companies, including Ferrari. When Ford met Allesandro DeTomaso, a race-car driver who was building his own cars, often using Ford engines, he saw an opportunity to combine beautiful Italian design with a powerful mid-engine American V-8. The car Ford visualized would also feature fully independent suspension and four-wheel disk brakes.

Eleven months after Ford and DeTomaso joined forces, the first Pantera, designed by Tom Tjaarda, rolled off the assembly line in Modena. Production began in 1971. Although the automobile was striking, with a sleek, low profile reflecting its Italian roots, a host of problems soon began to arise—overheating, brake problems, structural flaws, and complaints about creature comforts, to name a few.

The automotive press skewered the Pantera, reporting every glitch with glee. In 1975, faced with new fuel economy and emissions requirements that would have necessitated a major reengineering of the automobile, Ford ended its relationship with DeTomaso.

DeTomaso Automobili continued to build Panteras but was forbidden by its deal with Ford to export the car to the United States for ten years. The company solved most of the problems that plagued the original Panteras, and production continued on a limited basis until the early 1990s.

Kumpf was also a Rolls-Royce dealer, and, when it became apparent to the dealership's executives that the Pantera's days were numbered, Mitchell's boss asked him if he would be interested in learning how to work on Rolls-Royces. "I told him," Mitchell says, "you show me what one looks like, I can probably figure out how to work on them."

For the next two years, 1975 and 1976, Mitchell spent one week every month at a different United States dealer that sold and serviced Rolls-Royce. "There would be four or five guys in the class," he says, "and each dealer would

A 1993 PC-23. At the end of the 1991 season, Team Penske hired Nigel Bennett, who had worked at Lola, to design a new car. Although his PC-21 did not win the championship that year, it did show promise. In 1993, Bennett updated the car and produced the PC-22, powered by the new Chevy/C engine. A year later, he added aerodynamic modifications, new gear boxes, and the Ilmor V-8/d engine. In 1994, the Chevy was replaced with Mercedes-Benz power and Team Penske went on to capture the PPG Championship Cup. This car was driven by Al Unser Jr.

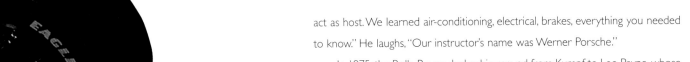

act as host. We learned air-conditioning, electrical, brakes, everything you needed to know." He laughs, "Our instructor's name was Werner Porsche."

In 1975, the Rolls-Royce dealership moved from Kumpf to Leo Payne, whose main business was selling Pontiacs. Since Rolls required that a dealer have a certified mechanic on staff, Mitchell moved too.

"It wasn't the best situation," he says. "I found out they were paying me fifty cents an hour less than the Mercedes mechanics. I immediately quit. When Rolls made a big fuss, I was rehired, with a raise." He shrugs, "I think they figured it was worth it when one of the Mercedes mechanics blew up a Rolls-Royce engine."

After three years with Leo Payne, Rolls-Royce was unhappy with the relationship and awarded the dealership to Royal Carriage Works. "Bill Stewart owned the shop," Mitchell says. "He was an independent, much like I am today, and worked on BMWs, Ferraris, stuff like that."

After he had been at the new shop for about a week, Mitchell was visited by the police. The officer explained that Mitchell's previous employer had accused him of stealing Rolls-Royce tools, showing him a detailed, six-page list of the "missing" items. Mitchell called Walter Bell, the Rolls-Royce rep, who brought an identical list to police headquarters. Bell explained that the list included every tool mandated by Rolls-Royce for an authorized dealer, including a 100-ton press—a difficult item to stick in a lunch box.

Mitchell chuckles, "The police figured things out, and, from what I heard, heads rolled at Leo Payne."

After a short time at Royal Carriage Works, Mitchell left and was making plans to seek another career when he got a phone call. "A Rolls-Royce owner called me at home," he says. "I had taken care of his car, and he needed some work done. I told him that I didn't have cash for parts and he told me, 'I didn't ask about

Roger Penske is aware of the fact that his cars make up the majority of Mitchell's collection, but Mitchell has no idea how Penske feels about it. "From what I've been told," Mitchell says, "Mr. Penske doesn't live in the past and isn't real big on memorabilia. He is concerned with today's race, not what happened two or three years ago."

Other Penske cars in Mitchell's collection include the PC-17, a machine that won more races than any other Penske car, and the PC-21, Mitchell's favorite. "That was Rick Mears's last car," says Mitchell. "Rick Mears has always been one of my favorite drivers."

Mitchell describes Mears as "the most unassuming man I have ever met. If you didn't know anything about what he accomplished on the track—he won the Indianapolis 500 four times!—you wouldn't learn anything new because he won't tell you. If you want to know about his career, you have to ask him. Even then, he's extremely modest."

Some of the drivers know about Mitchell's collection and stop by when they are in Denver. "We've had Danny Sullivan, John Andretti, Rick Mears, and a few others in the shop," Mitchell says. "It's always fun to see them, and sometimes, if I happen to have a car that they personally drove, it can get a little emotional."

A number of Mitchell's cars are kept in his shop, along with his extensive collection of parts purchased when England's March Racing went out of business. "They built all types of race cars," Mitchell says, "and, as the British say, they went into receivership."

Mitchell heard through the grapevine that all of March's parts were for sale and purchased its entire inventory. He smiles, "That stuff was worth millions. Believe me, I paid a lot less than that."

Not only have the hard-to-find parts been useful for his own projects, but Mitchell has put together a nice little business selling parts to other racers. "We have customers calling us every day," he says, gesturing at the extensive racks that fill an entire room in the shop. "Vintage racers, race teams restoring older cars, museums, anybody who needs parts for Indy cars. They are looking for wishbones, uprights, bobbins, things like that. We are one of the few places that have them."

The rest of Mitchell's cars are displayed in a private museum in a Boulder, Colorado, office building. The high-tech environment is a perfect match for the colorful machines. One car, located on the second floor, is especially elegant. Painted in prism, the latest trend in automotive paint, the car's surface actually appears to change color as you walk by. With all of the product endorsements eliminated from the body, you can really appreciate the elegant, functional lines of the root-beer-colored, four-wheel chameleon.

One of the interesting non-Penske machines in Mitchell's collection represents Porsche's second attempt to assault the Indy 500. After several years of reconnaissance, Porsche unveiled its entry for the 1980 Indy 500 to the American racing press on December 11, 1979. The car was built by Interscope

While we were photographing Mitchell's cars, Phil Hill happened to stop by to see the collection. Hill, the first American to win the World Championship in Formula 1, also won the 24 Hours of LeMans and 12 Hours of Sebring three times each.

and powered by a turbocharged flat-six developed from the engine used in the Porsche 935.

Unfortunately, Porsche's arrival at Indy coincided with the year the United States Auto Club (USAC) and CART were getting divorced. USAC, hoping to promote the use of cheaper, production-based power plants, reduced the boost that could be used on turbochargers. When testing proved that the car would not be competitive, Porsche pulled the plug. The undertaking, however, was not for naught. The engine from the stillborn Indy program was the basis for the power plant that Porsche installed in the cars that dominated Le Mans during the 1980s.

In 1987, Porsche again entered the Indianapolis arena. Power was supplied by a V-8 designed by Hans Mezger. The chassis was originally built in-house, but poor performance convinced Porsche to switch to March-built machines.

After three lackluster years, Porsche withdrew from Indy racing in 1990. Its lone victory was won by Teo Fabi at Mid-Ohio in 1989. Painted in its original Quaker State green livery, Fabi's winning car was purchased by Mitchell in 1990.

Porsche offered Mitchell an engine for the car—if he bought all ten of them! "The engine wasn't that good," Mitchell says. "Its lack of power was the major reason the cars didn't do that well. The only reason I wanted one was the fact that it was original to the car. I certainly didn't want ten, so I passed." The car is now powered by a Cosworth/Ford.

Talking about future acquisitions, Mitchell is not very optimistic. Collectors are faced with the harsh reality that many race cars are destroyed. A race team has only so much room to spare for storing older machines, and nostalgia does not pay the bills.

"It's a numbers game," Mitchell says. "They don't make that many of them. A good example is the '92 Penske cars. If I'm not mistaken, there were eight of them built, and today there are only four left. We have three of them."

Mitchell's Penske PC-12 is really unique. "It's the only one in the world," he says. "Serial number one, that's the one in our collection. Serial number two was destroyed during testing in England. Serial number three was never finished, and what was put together ended up at Rick Mears's house. He used it to recuperate after he sustained massive foot injuries when he wrecked at Sanair Super Speedway near Montreal in 1984. He would sit in it and work his feet." Mitchell laughs, "The car ended up being a very expensive therapy machine."

He continues, "The last PC-12, serial number four, was given to a university in England. The engineering department destroyed the car while they were testing it to see what kind of twisting motions it could take before it failed."

Over the years, many Indy cars have simply disappeared. A few years ago, Mitchell sold a bunch of cars to a party in Japan. "At this point," he says, "nobody seems to have any idea what happened to them."

Although four of his cars can be driven, Mitchell has been unable to take them out to the track for several years. During renovations on his new shop, a 1,500-pound beam was dropped on Mitchell's left foot. He ended up losing several toes and the feeling in the rest.

"I've gotten down in the cars, sat in them," he says, "I can't feel the clutch or brake. A lot of drivers use the right foot for both braking and the gas pedal. It's called heel and toe. I never could master that, so I use my left foot to brake and keep my right foot on the gas. The clutch isn't that much of a problem, but I can't feel how much pressure I'm putting on the brakes. I am afraid I would stomp on them and end up hitting the wall, or worse. It's too dangerous to take the chance."

Although he's hurting, Mitchell has not given up. He has built several "shifter" go-karts and hopes that some hot laps in them will get him back in the Indy cars. These superkarts are a far cry from the crude machines, with a Briggs & Stratton or a Clinton four-cycle lawn-mower engine, that I drove around parking lots in the 1950s. Powered by motorcycle engines, and utilizing five- or six-speed gearboxes, shifter karts are capable of top speeds in excess of 125 mph.

Even if he never gets behind the wheel of one of his Indy cars again, Mitchell knows he has been fortunate. "There are thousands of guys who would love to get into an Indy car, go out on a track, and play with it." He turns and looks at the PC-23. "I've been extremely lucky because I've been able to drive them to my heart's content."

Gil Nickel

In 1945, Harold and Rebecca Nickel opened Greenleaf Nursery in Muskogee, Oklahoma. Gil Nickel was six years old, and his brother, John, ten. "Dad told us," Gil Nickel says, "that if John and I wanted to continue eating, we would have to learn how to work. The nursery was a cash-and-carry operation, and I worked there after school and on weekends. It was a real family business." During the 1950s, the Nickels began to experiment with growing plants in containers, and, in 1957, they purchased 570 acres, thirty-five miles east of Muskogee on Lake Tenkiller. That same year, Nickel graduated from high school and enrolled at Baylor University in Waco, Texas. After two years, he transferred to Oklahoma State. "I majored in physics and math," he says. "That was the Sputnik era, and I wanted to help get us to the moon."

Institute of America), the Gustav Niebaum Winery (today's Niebaum-Coppola), and Chateau Montelena.

In addition to his skills as an architect, McIntyre invented the gravity-flow winery. Grapes would be delivered to the top-floor level and from there fall into the crusher. The crushed grapes would then continue their descent to the bottom level, where they would begin the fermentation process. "Today," Nickel says, "there are other energy sources available to move the product. We have changed the layout of the winery to take advantage of new technology."

The name Benson chose for his winery, Far Niente, is taken from an Italian proverb, *Dolce far niente*—"It's sweet to do nothing." When Nickel purchased the building he found the words "Far Niente" chiseled into a stone wall. "Who was I to change it?" he says. "It refers to the time of the day or part of your life when you decide to do what you like to do best. Far Niente does not mean you sit around and do nothing. It's the time you spend putting your life into perspective."

The early Far Niente winery prospered, but Prohibition put it out of business, as it did so many other purveyors of "strong drink." During the 1920s the owners simply walked away, and the stone buildings began to slowly decay.

Nickel is obviously blessed with a very good imagination because Far Niente was a hulk when he bought it. "The building was so dilapidated," he says, "I could stand on the third floor and see clear down to the barrel room in the cellar." Floors, walls, and ceilings were missing, and there were no doors or windows in the structure. Birds and other assorted wildlife were the only tenants in residence.

Nickel hired Gene Domenicelli and Sons to restore the stonework on the main building, a job that took an entire year to complete. T&O Masonry, a firm with headquarters in nearby St. Helena, restored the winery's fireplaces, going so far as to duplicate the cut stones on the building's exterior. Since there were no doors or windows to use as models, architect Ron Nunn designed replacements that are in keeping with the style of those that would have been installed when the structure was built.

Nickel has added forty thousand square feet of underground caves, where Far Niente's wines are aged in wooden barrels. "The taste of the great wines," he says, "is due in part to the traditional process of aging wine in small wooden barrels, so I decided to do the same." After experimenting with several types of wood, Nickel discovered that the taste he wanted to achieve was only possible by using barrels made from the wood found in three French forests: Allier, Bourgogne, and Nevers. "We also hand pick and sort all of our grapes," Nickel says. "I think this is the mark of a great winery because hand sorting makes it possible to make excellent wine in a difficult year." Far Niente wines are renowned for their ability to age gracefully, and the Cave Collection allows for the limited release of wines for a number of years after the vintage.

Nickel originally estimated the restoration would take a year. It ended up being a three-year labor of love and costing $4 million—on top of the half-million he paid

Built in 1885, Far Niente was founded by John Benson, a colorful character who struck it rich during the California gold rush. Prohibition put the winery out of business, and the owners simply walked away. The stone buildings were slowly sinking into decay until discovered by Gil Nickel in 1979.

for the building and thirteen surrounding acres. "Thank God," he says, "we didn't know in advance how long it was going to take or how much it was going to cost."

Nickel produced his first wine while Far Niente was still under restoration. The grapes were crushed at a Napa Valley winery, and the juice was then hauled to a warehouse in Sausalito for fermentation.

Far Niente's debut was a 1979 Chardonnay. "It caused quite a stir," Nickel says. "Right from the start, I wanted to do everything the right way. We used gold foil on the label. Fifteen dollars a bottle was pretty steep in those days for a California wine."

Nickel may have been the first modern-day California vintner to seal his entire production in wooden cases. "Cardboard never seemed right for fine wine," Nickel says. Mary Marshall Grace, Far Niente's director of communications, says, "I still meet people today who remember the labels and the packaging from that time. They comment on the attention that Far Niente attracted." She smiles, "I think that Gil was simply ahead of the curve."

If Nickel was going to make the distinguished wine he envisioned, he knew he needed to learn as much as he could about the art of winemaking. He enrolled at the University of California at Davis and spent a year studying enology and viticulture. "Those courses," Nickel says, "helped me understand the physics and chemistry of winemaking. I also read all the books on the subject that I could find and visited wineries, both in Europe and California. I wanted to see for myself how successful vintners were doing things."

Far Niente produces only three wines: a Chardonnay, a Cabernet Sauvignon, and a Dolce, an elegant dessert wine. Both the Chardonnay and the Cabernet are blended from various estate vineyards to create wines that, as Nickel explains it, "capture the recognizable Far Niente house style."

The result of three years' labor and $4 million: Far Niente's stately buildings and grounds reflect Gil Nickel's vision and attention to detail. "Thank God," he says, "we didn't know in advance how long it was going to take, or how much it was going to cost."

Nickel drifts through a corner in his 1972 Formula 2 Surtees at Road America in Wisconsin. The legendary Mike Hailwood was driving the Matchbox Special when he won the European Formula 2 Championship in 1972.

Right: Love that Marlon Brando hat. Nickel rode a BMW motorcycle while he was going to college. "The local Ford dealership had taken it in from some kid for a trade on a new convertible," he says. "It had 20,000 miles on it when I bought it, and I sold it eleven years later with 120,000 miles. That motorcycle never once broke down

Nickel & Nickel plans to eventually produce twenty-five different wines. In addition to Napa Valley Cabernets, the list includes Chardonnay, Merlot, and a Russian River Valley Zinfandel.

Gil Nickel's attention to quality, style, and history are singular. Far Niente wines consistently score in the nineties on *Wine Spectator*'s 100-point scale, and Nickel's restoration of the winery earned Far Niente a place on the National Register of Historic Places.

Excellence also costs money. "We are," Nickel says, "at or near the top of the pyramid." A bottle of Far Niente Chardonnay costs about $50, and a Cabernet will set you back $100. The wines produced by Nickel & Nickel range between $35 and $125.

In addition to his quest to make great wine and collect noteworthy auto-mobiles, Nickel craves speed. When he was showing his cars at the Pebble Beach Concours d'Elegance, he began to hear guys talking about vintage racing. "It sound-ed interesting," he says, "and a lot more exciting than the concours thing. The con-cours is a lovely event—great for the oldsters and their collector cars and picnic hampers—but a little too quiet for me." The more Nickel learned about vintage racing, the more he wanted to try it.

"Starting in 1983," he says, "I'd drive my 340 America to Sears Point [now Infineon Raceway, in Sonoma County, California], and spread my tools out on the ground. I was chief driver, mechanic, and bottle washer, trying to learn how it was done. It turned out that I didn't know anything about racing." He smiles, "You might think you are a pretty good driver on the street, but it has nothing to do with actually racing a car."

The Vintage Sports Car Club (VSCC), founded in England in 1934, was the first known organization to race sports cars that were at least five years old. At about the same time in the United States, two brothers, Sam and Miles Collier, formed the Automobile Racing Club of America (ARCA). The Colliers, whose father made a fortune in streetcar advertising and real estate, were major fans of early MGs. Emulating the "European" style of racing, the Colliers hosted events for fellow enthusiasts at their Pocantico Hills estate in Westchester County, New York.

Although World War II brought racing to an abrupt halt, the war exposed American servicemen to English and European sports cars. When they returned home, many ex-GIs bought Jaguars, MGs, Austin Healeys, and Porsches, and were soon looking for some action.

The ARCA changed its name to the Sports Car Club of America (SCCA) and held events at Watkins Glen and Bridgehampton, both in New York State. By the late 1950s technology had rendered many of the earlier cars obsolete and unable to compete with the newer machines. Finding themselves left in the dust, many owners sent their cars to the crusher or pulled the battery and parked them in the garage.

Those who lacked the deep pockets to step up to late-model iron, or simply enjoyed driving the earlier cars, found an opportunity to continue racing when the American version of the Vintage Sports Car Club (VSCC) was founded in 1959. That same year, the first VSCC event took place at Road America in Elkhart Lake, Wisconsin. As the cost of contemporary racing continued to escalate, vintage-racing clubs began to spring up all over the country. Competitors were attracted as much by the camaraderie of fellow racers as the opportunity to exercise their treasured automobiles.

In 1973, Steve Earle organized the first Monterey Historical Races, held the same weekend as the nearby Pebble Beach Concours. Vintage racing had arrived.

Today, vintage racing is the fastest-growing segment in motor sports. Many tracks have their best attendance on their vintage weekends, when a wide range of events, for almost every kind of race car, provides an opportunity for aficionados to experience the thrill of competition. Although the rules vary from club to club—some allow cars that were built yesterday—the cut-off for eligibility is usually cars built before 1972. The VSCC requires its cars to predate 1960.

In the United States, the sport has been described as "gentlemen's racing." In his book, *Vintage Racing! Start to Finish*, Jim McCarthy stated, "A vintage race event in the U.S. is nothing more than a moving classic car show at speed with friendly competition thrown in as an added attraction."

For many vintage racers, McCarthy's description may describe their deportment on the track, but Nickel is a bit more motivated. "This is my sport," he states emphatically. "I'm not playing tiddlywinks out there. We may be amateurs—we don't race for money—but the guys in the front know how to slide their cars and get the last ounce of speed out of them. At the front of the pack, it is always very competitive. The guy next to you may have a $5 million Ferrari, but that doesn't mean there is no contact. There's a lot of contact."

He continues, "It's a dream sport for a guy like me who has a need for speed. I love the cars, love the scene, and love the speed. I'm a safer driver on the streets since I took up vintage racing because I don't think I have to go as fast as I used to. I save my speed for the track, where all the cars are going in the same direction and there's no highway patrolman hiding behind a tree with a radar gun."

After his early below-par experiences at Sears Point, Nickel decided he could use some lessons. "I enrolled at Bob Bondurant's Racing School," he says. "I figured, tennis players take lessons, golfers take lessons, why shouldn't race-car drivers? I've probably been to a half-dozen driving schools over the years."

Nickel also realized that he needed a newer car. "Racing an early Ferrari is

Left: Two lovely examples of Colin Chapman's handiwork—a Lotus 27 Formula Junior and a Lotus 23B, painted in the Far Niente Team's distinctive livery. Produced in 1963, the 27 was Lotus's first monocoque Formula Junior car. Not especially successful when it was new—the bodywork had a habit of flexing—the car has benefitted from modern technology and is now extremely popular with vintage racers. The Type 23, produced from 1962 until 1964, was the last small-capacity pure sports racer designed by Colin Chapman. The car's performance was exceptional and it became known as "the giant killer." Nickel describes the 23B as "a strong car, without many maintenance problems. It's also an easy car to drive—sort of like driving a big go-kart."

Above: Nickel and the 23B in action at the 2003 Wine Country Classic Vintage Car Races.

rather like driving a John Deere tractor," Nickel says. "They go like the dickens, but they don't turn or stop very well."

During the late 1980s, he added a 1964 Lotus 26R, a 1962 Lotus 23B, and a 1972 Formula 2 Surtees to his stable of racers. The latter is the championship-winning Matchbox Special, driven by the legendary Mike Hailwood when he won the European Formula 2 Championship.

Seven years ago, Nickel married Beth Yorman. "Beth and I had known each other forever," he says. "She was my longtime sweetheart. Her family was also in the nursery business, and Beth's father was one of my father's first customers.

"In 1995," Nickel says, "Beth and I moved to Italy's Lake Como for the summer. We took Chris Chesbrough, my full-time crew chief, a mechanic, our truck, and a couple of race cars. Chris is a mechanical wizard and a can-do guy. I ended up winning the FIA European championship."

Chesbrough is a man of many talents. In addition to his duties at the racetrack, he is the captain of Nickel's eighty-five-foot, beautifully restored 1939 De Vries Lentsch motoryacht. "Chris is one of the youngest hundred-ton captains to ever be licensed by the Coast Guard," Nickel says. " He grew up on his parents' old sailing ship in the South Pacific."

Nickel believed that his Lotus 23 was the perfect car to race in the Historic Sports Car Class. He describes the 23 as "a strong car, without many maintenance problems. It's also an easy car to drive—sort of like driving a big go-kart."

Designed by the innovative genius Colin Chapman, the Lotus 23 became known as a "giant killer" after Jim Clark put on an incredible display at the Nurburg-Ring in Germany in 1962. Powered by a 1498cc, four-cylinder Lotus-Ford engine, the diminutive car ran away from everything on the track, including the best that Ferrari, Porsche, and Aston Martin had to offer, before mechanical problems forced Clark out of the race.

Later that year, the 23 was banned from running at Le Mans for reasons that had more to do with politics than mechanics. Infuriated, Chapman vowed to never again race at Le Mans. He kept his word.

Nickel's 23, which he bought in 1987, had been raced in Canada, where George Chapman, of Winnipeg, won the Canadian championship with the car in 1966. Thanks to Lotus specialist Dave Vegher, the car features a chrome-molly space frame and an engine that puts out almost 200 horsepower, double that of the original.

"During that summer in Europe," Nickel says, "of the thirty or forty cars entered in each race, most of them were Lotus 23s. The factory only built about 120 of them, and I think that nobody ever threw one away."

Adding to the challenge, Nickel had never seen, much less raced at, any of the tracks. "We usually didn't speak the language," he says. "Hell, we sometimes couldn't even find the starting grid. Nevertheless, out of the seven races, we only missed one because I had to come back home to take care of some business."

Of the six races Nickel started, he won four, finished third once, and broke down once. "That was the only breakdown we had all year," he says, "which is a credit to Chris. We were doing a lot of racing, and he kept the cars running. It all came down to the last race of the season in Burgundy, France. We had to win the last race to capture the championship, and ended up winning by half a car length. It was exhilarating."

When asked about future racing plans, Nickel hesitates for a moment before answering. "I'm getting a little long in the tooth for my sport. I just turned sixty-four, and my lips tremble when I say those words. I'm probably not going to buy any new cars because it makes sense for me to stick with the cars I am familiar with. Before long, maybe I'll be one of those guys in the back, moving over to let the leaders come through. I hate to think about that because I'm one of those people who believes, show me a good loser and I'll show you a good loser."

The good ship *Far Niente*, Nickel's eighty-five-foot, beautifully restored 1939 De Bries Lentsch motoryacht.

Epilogue

I interviewed Nickel several months before his death in October 2003. We met in his motor home during the 2003 Wine Country Classic Vintage Car Races.

Sponsored by *Wine Country Living*, the event, held at Infineon Raceway, featured more than two hundred vintage race cars. It was an undeniable thrill to see cars that I have only seen in photographs howling down the straightaways and sliding through the turns—instead of quietly reposing behind velvet ropes in a museum.

Harry Mathews had told me that the highlight of any event attended by Gil Nickel was the post-race festivities he hosted in his paddock. It was obvious that a lot of the race crowd felt the same way. Bounteous trays of appetizers appeared, but the reason for all the buzz was evident when Chris Chesbrough and his associates broke out their corkscrews. Far Niente wines were soon flowing freely. The reviews are right on: Gil Nickel's winery makes great wine.

As William and I were about to leave, we thanked Nickel for his hospitality and the chance to taste his products. I took the opportunity to ask one last question—Which does he enjoy most, making great wine or racing fast cars?

"When I'm going fast," he said, gesturing at the bright yellow cars parked in front of his trailer, "it would have to be the cars." Then, smiling, he studied the golden Chardonnay in his glass. "When I'm sitting still, I'll take the wine."

Gil and Beth Nickel touring the Austrian Alps in July 1994.

Malcolm Pray

When he was eleven years old, Malcolm Pray's parents took him to the 1939 New York World's Fair. Located on what was once a marshy wasteland in Flushing Meadow, the futuristic "World of Tomorrow," poised between the Depression and World War II, offered Americans a tangible vision of hope and prosperity in the face of uncertainty and confusion. "It was a wonderful age for me to go to the fair," he says. "I was interested in everything. I saw television, fiberglass, modern appliances, things that I had never seen before. My only regret is that I never got into the Futurama exhibit because the lines were too long." The young man might have missed the future as envisioned by General Motors, but he did see an automobile that captured his imagination and would fuel his passion for collecting.

An exhibit in the French Pavilion included several automobiles that showcased exceptional French custom coachwork. The vehicle that fascinated young Malcolm was a 1937 Delahaye 135M Cabriolet. The bodywork was designed and fabricated by the gifted coachbuilders Figoni et Falaschi, in collaboration with the artist Geo Ham. Ham was well known at the time for his futuristic automotive and aeronautical illustrations in the avant-garde French publication *L'Illustration*.

The car's most dramatic feature is its unique, swooping fenders, which the motoring press referred to as "les ailes [wings] Figoni." As many as forty-eight hand-hammered pieces of steel, butt-welded together section by section and then finished by hand with grinders, files, and sandpaper, were required to create each of those exquisite teardrops.

Emile Delahaye founded his company in 1845, in Tours, France. His first products were machines that made bricks. In 1894 he built his first cars, belt-driven and powered by small, single- or double-cylinder engines. Poor health forced Delahaye to retire in 1905; the company was purchased by Georges Morane. Charles Weiffenbach succeeded Delahaye as director of engineering, a position he would hold until 1954. The firm moved to Paris, built a new factory, and was soon producing an amazing array of vehicles and machinery: cars, trucks, industrial engines, fire vehicles, high-performance speedboats, agricultural equipment, and tanks.

In 1933 Delahaye, a company known for building dependable, but undistinguished, automobiles, decided to add luxury cars to its product line. Customers could order an automobile out of Delahaye's catalogue, or have the body custom-built by a coachmaker of their choice. The Coupe des Alpes and type 135 were introduced in 1934, powered by a potent overhead-valve, six-cylinder engine that produced 150 horsepower.

The Delahaye 135s were outfitted with some of the most fanciful bodywork ever seen on automobiles, created by a who's-who of the world's finest coachmakers. These included Figoni et Falaschi, Chapron, Labourdette, Pennock, Franay, and Worblaufen. Of these, the designs by Figoni et Falaschi are considered the most notable.

When asked about his automotive designs, Ovidio Falaschi replied, "We really were veritable couturiers of automotive coachwork, dressing and undressing a chassis one, two, three times and even more before arriving at the definitive line that we wanted to give to a specific chassis-coachwork ensemble."

Although at that time Mercedes-Benz and Auto Union were dominating sports-car racing, the Delahaye proved to be more than just a pretty face, performing admirably on the track. Delahayes soon became sought after by the rich and famous. Rita Hayworth drove a Delahaye, a gift from Prince Aly Khan, that featured hand-tooled leather crests and fleurs-de-lis inset into the seats and dashboard. El Glaoui, Pasha of Marrakesh, ordered one, and Clark Gable cut a dashing

Previous page: Malcolm and Natalie Pray with the 1937 Delahaye 135M Cabriolet, designed by the gifted coachbuilders Figoni et Falaschi in collaboration with the artist Geo Ham.

Left: A 1946 Chrysler Town & Country convertible parked in front of Pray's facility in Banksville, New York. In 1941 Chrysler introduced the wood-trimmed Town & Country station wagon, available in a six- or nine-passenger model. Following the war, Chrysler resumed production of the woody, but it was available only as a sedan or a convertible, paneled in mahogany and trimmed with white ash. The Town & Country's interior was posh, featuring wood trim combined with leather and color-coordinated carpets. The cars required additional maintenance to keep up the wood's appearance, and they were prone to squeaking. They also required a great deal of handwork on the assembly line due to the preparation and fitting of the wooden body parts. In 1947 the mahogany was replaced by decals, although the white ash remained. The last year for the wood-trimmed Town & Country was 1950.

Above: Pray Automobile Corporation in the mid-1960s. "I wasn't the first to discover Volkswagen," Pray says, "but I got on the bandwagon and rode the wave."

figure in his bright red 135. Sir Peter Ustinov remarked, "One drives, of course, an Alfa Romeo; one is driven in a Rolls-Royce; but one gives only a Delahaye to one's favorite mistress."

During World War II, Delahaye built military vehicles, and, when hostilities ceased, it resumed the production of automobiles. Sales suffered because of a combination of high price tags, postwar inflation, and dated technology. Delahaye only built seventy-seven cars in 1951; when the company was sold to Hotchkiss in 1954, the doors were closed on one of the world's most fascinating automakers.

After seeing the 135M at the World's Fair, Malcolm Pray was so impressed that he began to collect photographs of European cars and did several drawings of the car—which he still has—in his high-school mechanical drawing class. In 1964, he saw an ad in the *New York Times* offering a Delahaye for sale. "The car was at a used-car dealer on Long Island," he says. "I went out there on a Saturday morning, fell in love with the car, and bought it on the spot."

After owning the car for four years, Pray took it to Don Lefferts's shop in Ridgefield, Connecticut, where it received a ground-up restoration. "It took a year and a half," Pray says. "That restoration cost a bundle, but it was worth it."

The Delahaye was joined by other cars as Pray's collection grew, but he has always considered the 135 to be his crown jewel. "It was such a special car," he says, "but I never took it to any car shows." He shrugs, "I thought the Concours was for Ralph Lauren and those kinds of guys. The more you can spend on a car, the more prizes you win."

In 1994 Pray's friend Rich Gorman, the owner of Vantage Motorworks in Miami and the president of the Delahaye Club in America, suggested that Pray take his car to the Meadow Brook Concours d'Elegance. Held at the Dodge estate near Detroit, Meadow Brook is one of the world's premier events.

Delahaye was the featured car that year because the marque was celebrating its centennial. Convinced that this would be a memorable event, Pray acquiesced, took the car to Meadow Brook, and won a blue ribbon.

"At one point," Pray says, "a group of Frenchmen surrounded the car. They were very excited, gesturing, talking to each other. Then one of them came over to me and exclaimed, 'This is the missing car!' Everybody wanted to know everything I knew about the car's history."

In 1995, Pray was invited to bring the Delahaye to Paris for a Concours d'Elegance in the Parc de Bagatelle and to participate in a rallye after the show. The car was shipped by boat, and when it arrived—the first time it had been back in France—the Delahaye Club of Paris invited Malcolm and his wife, Natalie, to a dinner at the Saint James Club. A hit at the Concours, the Delahaye was awarded "La coup du coeur de la publique," the Peoples' Choice Award.

At one time owning a Packard was the symbol of success. In 1937, *Fortune* magazine wrote: "For a generation its luxurious cars had never carried lesser folk than rich invalids to their airings, diplomats to embassies, gangsters to funerals, stars to the studios, war lords through Chinese dust, heroes through ticker tape, heiresses across Long Island and Grosse Pointe." Presidents Warren G. Harding and Franklin D. Roosevelt rode in Packards, Norman Rockwell drove one, and drummer Gene Krupa owned a cream-colored model with red wheels. Pray's car is a stately 1930 Dual Cowl Phaeton.

adventures at Meadow Brook and in Europe were described by Natalie in her book, *Malcolm's French Mistress*: "Throughout this unique experience we were blessed with fair weather, had seen many highways and horizons, and enjoyed harmony in motion. The Delahaye's endurance and reliability on the road, plus performance as an award-winning car and Concours star, was the ultimate in automotive grace under pressure."

Malcolm Sheldon Pray Jr. was born in Manhattan on November 22, 1928, and spent his early years on that island. Malcolm's father, an executive in the textile industry, could trace his family back to the Mayflower's John and Priscilla Alden.

The Pray family, like so many others, was hit hard by the Depression. "My father's company almost went out of business," Pray says, "and my mother's father owned a company that went down the tubes. Just about everything went down the tubes."

He continues, "That's why I treasured my toys. My erector set, my toy soldiers, toys that I still have today. I think it was those dark days that turned me into a collector. We had a 1939 Ford, and that car had to last us through World War II because you couldn't get another one. I contrast that with people today who treat cars as disposable items. Just tear it up, toss it in the junkyard, and go out and get a new one."

When Pray was in the fourth grade, his family moved to Bronxville. "Two years later," Pray says, "my father rented a house in Greenwich, and I have lived in Greenwich ever since."

Not long after his family moved to Connecticut, Pray discovered the Boy Scouts and cars. Both would have a significant influence on his later life. "I joined Troop 2 in Riverside, and we'd go on overnight bicycle trips to places that, at the time, seemed like wilderness."

Almost as soon as he arrived in Greenwich, Pray was a fixture in local automobile dealers' showrooms. "I loved the illustrated brochures and catalogues that described the new cars," he says. "I collected as many of them as I could, and the walls of my room were covered with pictures of cars."

Pray was so enthralled with automobiles that his family worried it might become an obsession. His cousin, Roberta Carr, was "amazed that he had pictures of cars instead of girls in his billfold." A family friend remembers the day Malcolm's mother confided her concerns. "Oh, I just don't know what I'm going to do about Malcolm. The only thing he thinks about is cars, cars, cars."

Although Malcolm did not graduate from high school, a family friend pulled some strings to get him accepted at the University of Virginia. Pray's career at that institution was less than stellar. "I spent four years there," he says, "and managed to pass one course a year. In those days, you could bluff your way through, and I was a hell of a bluffer. Needless to say, I never graduated."

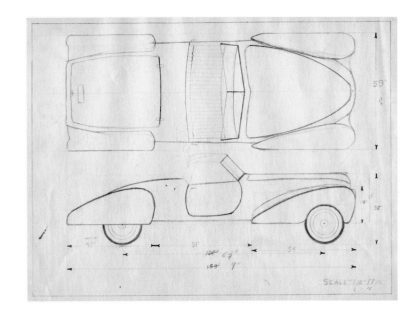

Left: From the top, a 1939 Lagonda V-12 Tulipwood Body Tourer, a 1935 Amilcar Pegase Grand Prix, a 1936 Auto Union (Audi) Wanderer, a 1938 Jaguar SS 100, and a 1937 Delahaye 135M.

Right: Malcolm Pray saw the Delahaye 135M at the 1939 New York World's Fair. He was so taken with the car that he made several drawings of it in his high school mechanical drawing class. In 1964 Pray bought a Delahaye at a Long Island used car dealer, and in 1995 discovered that the car was the same Delahaye that had thrilled him in 1939.

While he was at the university, Pray met John Frankenheimer, a filmmaker who would go on to direct *The French Connection*, *The Manchurian Candidate*, and *Seven Days in May*. "John talked me into joining the Air Force," Pray says, smiling. "He told me that he could get me an assignment as a photographer."

Pray ended up at the Cambridge Air Force Base Research Center in Massachusetts. "It was the beginning of the National Aeronautics and Space Administration, NASA," he says. "I got assigned to the accounting department and only had to work three or four days a week."

While stationed in Cambridge, Pray dated Natasha Boissevain. Her step-father, J. Russell Maguire, a wealthy Greenwich businessman, was less than thrilled with the young airman. In spite of her parents' objections, Natasha and Malcolm managed to carry on a relationship.

In 1955, Pray was discharged and returned to Greenwich. His father suggested that he get a job in Manhattan in banking, the stock market, or advertising—"an appropriate career for a young man." Pray remembers, "My father would get on the train at seven in the morning. When he arrived in New York, he would have to ride the subway downtown, and that was before the cars were air-conditioned. Then, he wouldn't get home until seven at night. I saw how unhappy my father was with that life and I was determined that it wasn't going to happen to me."

Instead of taking the New Haven railroad into Manhattan, Pray went to work selling cars. "I saw the 1955 Packard Request in a showroom window on the Post Road," he says. "I was like a rat drawn to a big piece of cheese."

The car that seduced Pray was Packard's one-off "dream car" for 1955. Designed by Richard Teague at the "request" of Packard's loyal customers for a car that echoed Packard's glory years, the pearl white and copper car featured a formal vertical radiator flanked by two horizontal half-bumpers. The parking lights were located in bomblike projections, which were soon known as "Dagmars."

Pray was offered a summer job at the Packard dealership, with a salary of fifty dollars a week and a draw on commission. "I didn't even know what the hell a draw on commission meant," he says, "but I remember my father's reaction to

my new job. He practically had apoplexy." After a summer selling Packards, Pray went to work for Morlee Motors, a foreign-car dealership in Greenwich, owned by Harry Blanchard. It was in Morlee Motors' showroom that Pray found his calling. "I finally discovered something I was good at. I wasn't very good in school, I wasn't a great athlete, and I didn't set the world on fire in the Air Force. But I could sell cars." He smiles, "I think I was a good salesman because I would stand there and let the customers talk themselves into the car. Then I would tweak the close, and get them out the door and into the car."

Pray also understood how to go the extra mile. "A couple came in and they were looking at an MG," he says. "They wanted to take a test drive but didn't have anybody to watch their baby." The young salesman ended up going to their house to take care of the infant while the couple drove around Greenwich in the MG. "I didn't know much about babies," Pray says. "While they were gone, I said, 'Kid, you'd better not queer this sale for me.' He didn't."

Now that he had a job, Pray proposed to Natasha, and they were married at the Maguire home on October 27, 1956. They moved into a small rented house, and their first child, Sabrina, was born two years later.

In the 1950s, a foreign-car dealership sold everything. In addition to Volkswagen and Porsche, Morlee Motors handled most of the cars being imported into the United States: MG, Austin Healey, Jaguar, Hillman, Morris, Fiat, Alfa Romeo, Lancia, and Mercedes. "In those days," Pray says, "it was every man for himself. A guy would rent a shop, order a couple of Jaguars, and he was a dealer."

Within two years Pray was Morlee Motors' sales manager, and two years later he was promoted to general manager. In 1960 Blanchard was killed while racing a Porsche in Argentina, and his widow agreed to let Pray run the business, now called Blanchard-Pray Automobile.

Several years earlier, Pray had decided that the dealership's future lay with Volkswagen. "Volkswagen realized early on," he says, "that service was the key to success. People would buy a foreign car, go through the agony of trying to get it serviced or repaired, sell it in a couple of years, and vow never to buy another one. Volkswagen insisted that dealers set up separate facilities to service

Left: A lawn full of sports cars. From the top, a 1931 MG M-type boattail, a 1955 MG TF, a 1946 MG TC, a 1957 Porsche Speedster, a 1953 Jaguar XK 120, a 1961 Ferrari 250 GTO, a 1957 Thunderbird, a 1960 Mercedes 300SL, a 1961 Jaguar E-Type, a 1950 Allard J2X, a 1957 BMW 507, and a 1959 Chevrolet Corvette.

Above: The DeLorean was John DeLorean's attempt to build what he called an "ethical" sports car, featuring a stainless-steel body. Funding came from the British government, and a factory was built in Belfast, Ireland. However, production glitches led to customer complaints, and the automotive magazines gave the car lukewarm reviews. The early 1980s found DeLorean with serious financial problems, and the automaker was videotaped taking part in a $24 million cocaine deal in an attempt to save his beleaguered company. Two years later he was acquitted of all charges, but his credibility, along with his car, were ruined. Pray's car was built in 1982.

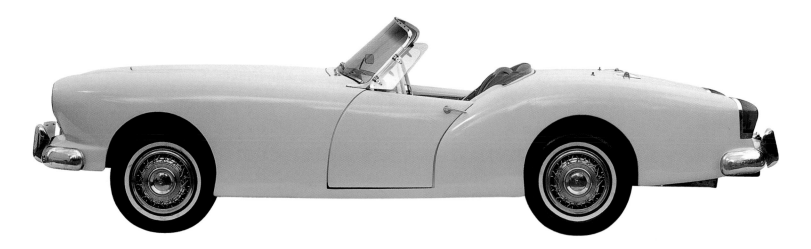

their cars. They wanted their customers to be happy."

Even though Blanchard-Pray Automobile already sold Volkswagen, Blanchard's death put that relationship in jeopardy. "I was young," Pray says, "and didn't have much in the way of financial resources. But I was able to convince Volkswagen that I had all the money I needed, and I convinced the bank that I had Volkswagen in my pocket. Both of them probably knew it wasn't true, but they were willing to go with my enthusiasm."

He laughs, "My outboard motorboat and '59 Chevy were my $2,100 investment. The rest was borrowed."

If timing is everything, it certainly paid off for Pray and his faith in Volkswagen. He picks up a model VW bug sitting on his desk. "I wasn't the first to discover Volkswagen, but I got on the bandwagon and rode the wave."

In 1964 Pray bought out Mrs. Blanchard, and the dealership became Pray Automobile. The demand for Volkswagens soon had him buying land adjacent to the business. On his fortieth birthday, November 22, 1968, Pray celebrated the grand opening of his new facility—four times the size of the original dealership.

When Audi made the decision to enter the American market in 1969, Pray Automobile was its first dealership in the country. Among his collection of memorabilia, Audi's "Letter of Intent 1" is one of Pray's most treasured possessions.

As customers lined up to buy Volkswagens at his dealership, Pray was able to purchase a large Colonial home on eight acres, a few miles from downtown Greenwich, on Round Hill Road. The Prays—who by then had three daughters, Sabrina, Melanie (called Lilly), and Natasha (called Tina)—moved into their new home on May 14, 1965. A son, Malcolm III, was born on May 13, 1969.

His business success also allowed Pray to begin collecting cars, and he built a large garage for the automobiles. Lilly, who Pray calls "my car daughter," remembers those days. "After he bought the Delahaye," she says, "he bought two or three cars a year, mainly European or sports cars." She laughs, "He built a ten-car garage that he fit twelve cars into. Dad has a way of parking cars like no one else."

All of the Pray children learned how to drive when they were ten. "We'd drive around the lawn in the dune buggy," Lilly says. "Dad was very rigorous in his training, and today I can drive just about anything." Lilly works as a firefighter in Boulder, Colorado. The day she had to parallel park a fire truck, she called her father. "I told him, 'You won't believe what I just did.'"

In 1977, Malcolm and Natasha separated, and they were divorced two years later. Natasha remarried, and Malcolm moved back into the Round Hill home.

After spending fifteen years as one of Greenwich's most eligible bachelors, Malcolm met Natalie Thomas. Born in Australia, Natalie was a career diplomat in the Australian foreign service, working at the United Nations in New York. They were married on December 2, 1995. Natalie has written two books detailing Malcolm's love affair with cars, and is currently working on a third.

On July 25, 1986, young Malcolm was killed in an automobile accident, a tragedy that shattered the entire family. "My brother's death devastated my father," Lilly says. "He was going to take over the business, conquer the world. It was a terrible time for all of us, and dad lost all interest in everything, including the car collection. They just sat there."

Lilly credits her sister Sabrina's ex-husband, Arno Fischer, for renewing her father's passion for his cars. "Arno," she says, "began to take my father to auctions and concours, things he had never done before. During the late 1980s and early 1990s, Dad really started to collect, and you know what he has today." Today, Pray keeps his cars—he has almost ninety and counting—in seven garages on the Round Hill property and at another facility in Banksville, a small town located in New York, a few minutes' drive from his home.

Pray maintains that you have to have three things to collect cars: passion, money, and space. "There are a lot of guys who have passion and money," he says, "but they don't have space. A guy will keep his cars in a warehouse, twenty miles from where he lives, and, if he's lucky, he will see his cars once a month. Also, you probably don't want to go there after dark. I'm lucky, I've got space."

The Kaiser Darrin, produced in 1953 and 1954, was designed by Howard "Dutch" Darrin, who had designed earlier cars for Kaiser-Frazer. Darrin built the prototype in his Hollywood studio, and, when he was satisfied, invited Henry Kaiser to see it. Kaiser was less than enthusiastic, but his new wife liked the car. Production began at a Kaiser-Frazer plant in Jackson, Michigan. The fiberglass body, built by GlasPar, a boat manufacturer, was mounted on a modified Henry J chassis. Power was provided by a Willys-designed, sixty-horsepower, six-cylinder F-Head engine. The Darrin's doors slid into the front fender, a novel feature that made it difficult to get in and out of the car and also proved to be a maintenance headache. Sales were limited by a high price tag—$10,000—tepid performance, and lack of customer faith in Kaiser-Frazer's future. Only 435 Darrins were produced.

Pray adds, "I'm an emotional collector. I buy cars because I like them. I don't buy them as an investment, and I don't care if anybody else likes them." He will often buy a car to fill a niche. "I bought the Rolls Phantom I last winter," he says, "because I wanted it to fit with the Phantom II, III, and V."

Several of Pray's cars remind him of his early years in Greenwich. "When I was a kid," he says, "I'd see them running around town and thought they were wonderful. Cars like the 1941 Cadillac, the 1941 Packard Darrin, and the 1940 Lincoln Continental Cabriolet."

Pray has a special affection for his Lincoln Continental because it was involved in what he describes as "a shipwreck." During August 1997, Pray shipped the car to Europe for the Paris Concours d'Elegance. "Natalie and I were at a hotel in Munich," he says, "when I got a phone call. They had opened up the container, and, according to the guy on the phone, the car was 'slightly damaged.'"

When he arrived in London, Pray discovered that sometime during the trip the container had obviously been dropped. "At first glance," he says, "it didn't look that bad. The body wasn't any worse than you'd expect from a fender bender. Then, I noticed that the wheels were splayed out." Upon closer examination, it turned out that not only were the Lincoln's frame and axles bent, the engine block and transmission were in several pieces.

Above: Malcolm and Natalie Pray driving the Delahaye 135M during the 1995 rallye organized by the Automobile Club of France. "The Delahaye drives like a dream," Pray says. "Of all my prewar cars, it has the best handling."

Left: Classic iron. Middle row, from the top: a 1941 Packard Darrin, a 1939 Lincoln Zephyr, a 1937 Cord 812, a 1941 Cadillac, and a 1934 Packard LeBaron Dual Cowl Phaeton. Top right, a 1934 Boattail Speedster. Left, a 1930 Duesenberg LeGrande Dual Cowl Phaeton. Below, a 1931 Cadillac Dual Cowl Phaeton.

In no shape to compete in a concours, the Lincoln was shipped back to the United States and underwent a full restoration at Bruce Amster's shop in Hyannis, Massachusetts. The car returned to Paris for the next year's event and won the award for Best Restoration. "I think it was the Paris persistence award," Pray says. "They all knew what happened to the car and had given it up for lost."

The Lincoln's restoration is a shameless example of Pray's emotional approach to collecting. "It cost about $80,000 to fix that car," he says. "I could have gone out and bought another one for a lot less money, but I didn't. I know this one is 100 percent perfect."

After running one of the country's most successful car dealerships for more than thirty-five years, Pray sold Pray Automobile in 1999. "I'm sorry now that I did it," he says, "but, at my age, it seemed like the right thing to do. Also, there was nobody in my family who wanted to be involved in the business."

Without spreadsheets and inventories to worry about, Pray has been able to concentrate on his many philanthropic and educational pursuits. After his son's death, Pray, remembering how much the Boy Scouts had meant to him while he was growing up, raised more than $400,000 to build the Malcolm S. Pray III Memorial Building in Greenwich. He is also involved with the Greenwich Chamber of Commerce, the American Red Cross, the Historical Society of the Town of Greenwich, and the Greenwich Boys and Girls Club.

He uses his cars as educational tools for his Malcolm Pray Foundation. "That's why I built Banksville. The best cars and my archives will be there for perpetuity. I have willed half of my car collection to the foundation to keep it going as an educational center for young people," he says. "I want to create that same spark in them that I got at the 1939 World's Fair."

Pray entertains groups of young people at Banksville, letting them get up close and personal with the cars. "That's the reason I bought the DeLorean," he says. "It was the car used in *Back to the Future*, and the kids can relate to it."

Lilly has seen some of the letters the children have sent to Malcolm. "They really appreciate what my father does," she says. "It gives them a chance to experience something they would otherwise never see. One girl, who was afraid she would never amount to anything, wrote and told my father that because of his interest in her, she is now going to college."

Every year, Greenwich holds a charity auction. One of the items up for bid is a tour of Pray's car collection. "We call it 'Cars and Cocktails,'" Pray says, "and it has brought as much as $6,000. The highest bidder gets cocktails and a tour of my car collection for himself and twenty friends. After everybody is gone, I go out to the garages to close up. It takes me about a half hour because I say good night to my beauties. If anybody heard me, they'd think I was wacko."

I have to admit that I have also talked to many of my cars, but it was usually when they were performing poorly, or not at all. I may have even gotten physical with one or two. I do not think Malcolm Pray is wacko. If I owned his cars, I would be talking to them all the time.

Above: The 1956 Lincoln Continental Mark II represented Ford's attempt to win back a major share of the high-end automotive market. The Continental's styling, described as "modern formal," was extremely clean for the chrome-plated mid-1950s. The car was practically hand-assembled, with the final finish requiring sixty hours of labor. Power was provided by Lincoln's 285 horsepower V-8 built with hand-selected parts. Initially the Continental sold well, but interest waned. Approximately 3,000 of the classy Mark IIs were built before production halted in May 1957.

Right, left to right: A 1899 horse-drawn wagon, a 1904 Metz Horseless Carriage, and a 1922 Renault Touring Town Car. In 1898, Charles Metz built a tandem bicycle equipped with a motor. The man in the rear would operate the motor and the rider in the front would steer. Metz went on to build a three-seater with two engines and advertised the machines as "Orient Motor-cycles." His famous ten-seater Orient bicycle is displayed at the Henry Ford Museum. Metz was also fascinated with automobiles; between 1903 and 1908, the Waltham Manufacturing Company of Waltham, Massachusetts, produced 2,500 Orient Buckboards.

Jon Shirley also collects automotive art. "I started collecting cars in the late 1980s," he says. "It was not a good time because the car market was very high. After the market collapsed, prices became more reasonable, and I began to collect postwar sports cars—Jaguars, Austin Healeys, MGs, Porsches, Mercedes, things like that."

Although Shirley had owned several Ferraris, it was not until he met Butch Dennison that he began to focus on Enzo's masterpieces. Dennison's company, Dennison International Motorsports, is located in Puyallup, an hour's drive south of Seattle. In addition to automotive restoration, Dennison provides track support for vintage racers.

"I didn't start off racing," Shirley says. "In 1994, Mary and I were invited to bring our 275GTS/4 NART spyder to Monterey. That was Ferrari's year at the Pebble Beach Concours d'Elegance. It was before I became involved with Butch, and I thought it would be a way to start off somewhere in the middle and learn the routine."

The Shirleys ended up taking the car to the Ferrari Nationals, three days before Pebble Beach. Although they did not win anything, the couple received

Previous page: Jon Shirley in his backyard with Alexander Calder's 1970 stabile *Red Curly Tail*. Jon and Mary Shirley are avid collectors of Calder's work and provided the funds to purchase the artist's stabile *Eagle*, a major work that is located in the Seattle Art Museum's Olympic Sculpture Garden.

Above: Jon and Mary Shirley at Willow Springs Raceway, Rosamond, California, in 1967.

Right: A 1969 Ferrari 312 Formula 1. This car was driven by Chris Amon and Pedro Rodriguez in three races during the 1969 season.

some positive feedback from the judges. Inspired, Jon and Mary spent the next three days feverishly working on the car, and they were awarded third in their class at the concours. "The two of us did all of the work on the car," he says, laughing. "In fact, Mary got fingernail fungus from all the polishing she did on the wire wheels. Third place meant a lot to two rank amateurs."

Since that first show, Shirley's cars have done extremely well. "I think we've had four firsts at Pebble," he says. "We've also won three of the world's most significant Ferrari awards. But, as I became more involved with Butch, vintage racing looked like it might be fun. Butch kind of talked me into it."

Shirley bought a Lotus 18, attended racing school, and began to compete in vintage events. "Today," he says, "I'm much more involved with vintage racing than restoring and selling."

Among the cars in Shirley's collection are seventeen Ferraris. Although Ferrari is considered to be the world's most famous sports-car manufacturer, the man behind the machine was interested in one thing: building winning race cars.

The main objective of automobile manufacturers has always been to build cars and sell them. Factory-sponsored racing might add some panache to a brand's image, but it has never been a major consideration. Ferrari saw it differently. He built race cars, and, when those cars won, he used that success to sell detuned versions of the cars to a lucky, well-heeled few.

Shirley's Ferraris represent a cross section of outstanding examples. His 1949 166MM Barchetta, which translates to "little boat," was one of three built for that year's racing season. The car's clean styling and outstanding performance on the track had much to do with establishing the Ferrari legend.

In 1953, Ferrari built three 340 America Coupes, with bodies by Pinin Farina. When the cars proved to be not as fast as Ferrari had hoped, they were returned to the factory and the engines were bored to 4.5 liters—375MM specifications. Pinin Farina modified the cars' bodies, giving each a new front-end treatment and a smaller rear window. Shirley bought his car in 1998 and has driven it in the Colorado Grand, the Mille Miglia 2000 in Italy, and the California Mille 2001.

Shirley also owns a 1954 375MM Scaglietti Coupe that was originally purchased by Roberto Rossellini. The legendary film director, who owned several Ferraris, inherited his love of the cars from his aunt, the Baronessa (Maria) Antonietta Avanzo. A personal friend of Enzo Ferrari, the baronessa was an enthusiastic driver who raced in a bright red jump suit that matched her Ferrari. When, in later life, her son demanded that she give up racing, she relented and took up big-game hunting.

Rossellini talked about producing a film that would document Italy's great racing champions: Fangio, Farina, Ascari, and Villoresi. He even entered the Mille Miglia, hoping to experience the sensations of racing for himself. After finishing less than half the course in last place, he gave up. The film was never made.

One of only four made, this 1956 Ferrari 290MM has an important racing history, including first place at the 1957 Nassau Trophy. The car was also Stirling Moss's first Ferrari drive. Other drivers who raced the car include Dan Gurney, Phil Hill, and Juan-Manuel Fangio.

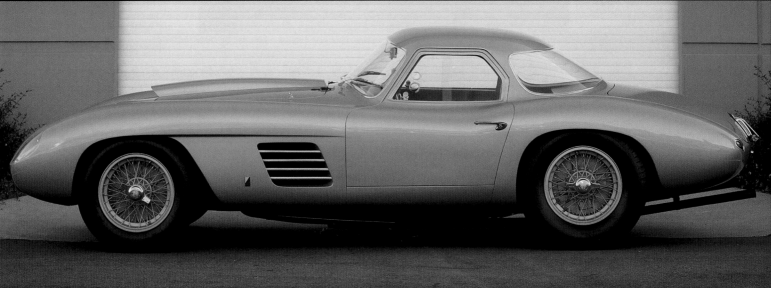

Roberto Rosellini owned this 1954 Ferrari 375 MM until 1964, when he sold it to a man in Sicily. In 1970, it was found in a barn in Palermo in terrible condition and pur-chased by a M. Robert from Paris. It remained in pieces from 1970 to 1995, when it was purchased by Jon Shirley. The car was sent to Pete Lovely Racing in boxes, and the restoration was completed in May 1998.

Right: The car's functional interior. Sergio Scaglietti opened his coachworks in 1951 and went on to design many of Ferrari's most stunning cars. Scaglietti was one of the few individuals who Enzo Ferrari considered a close friend.

Top: One of only two built, the little blue 1954 Ferrari Mondial 500 coupe's coachwork was created by Pinin Farina. The car, owned for forty-five years by a French collector before Shirley acquired it, has never been restored. Occasionally it is refreshing to see an original car amid all the polished splendor.

Bottom: A 1967 Ferrari 275 GTS/4 NART Spyder. Of the ten 275s built, only two cars, including this example, were fitted with aluminum bodies. Considered the rarest street "production" Ferrari, the car is used by Jon and Mary Shirley for long-distance rallyes. "It is a great driver," Shirley says. "The 275 was also the first Ferrari street car to be equipped with twin overhead camshafts."

Right: The 275GTS/4 was originally built as a closed car. Luigi Chinetti, North American Racing Team (NART) boss and Ferrari's distributor for the eastern United States, thought his customers would prefer to drive a sportier car. He arranged for a limited number of spyder versions to be built, which became known as the 275GTS/4 NART Spyders.

ing a free reel of recording tape if a customer came in and bought a reel." The promotion proved so popular that Shirley had to hire three additional employees.

While he was wiring the sound room in the San Leandro store, Shirley met Mary Johanson. "She was the girlfriend of the man I hired as assistant manager. We were married a year and a half later."

Shirley was soon promoted to district manager for Southern California and spent the next two and a half years opening up twenty-four new stores. "Then," he says, "the company asked me to move back to Boston because they wanted me to become involved in merchandising. I talked to Charles, and in his usual grumpy manner he told me there was more money in running the stores, but the company wanted me in Boston."

Shirley moved back East and was soon a frequent flyer to China, Taiwan, and Japan. "I bought just about everything that RadioShack sold," he says. "Stereo equipment, parts, kits, antennas. You name it, I bought it."

When Tandy announced that he was going to move RadioShack's headquarters to Fort Worth in 1971, not everybody in Boston was happy. The move was much less traumatic for Mary and Jon Shirley. "I was now merchandise manager in charge of all product lines, and we found a nice house on Eagle Mountain Lake.

We bought a boat, we had a boathouse," he says. "It was wonderful."

In 1973, Tandy decided he wanted to move into the European market. "He asked me if I would be one of the four guys who would go to Europe and start the thing up," Shirley says. "I was the first to go."

Shirley rented office space in Brussels, which became the company's European headquarters, and helped open stores in France, Belgium, Holland, Germany, and England. "I had a multilingual staff," he says, "We were responsible for the merchandising and advertising for all the countries we had stores in." He laughs, "In Germany, we had to call them Tandy Stores because RadioShack translates literally as 'cheap chicken coop.'"

After five and a half years in Europe, Shirley moved back to Fort Worth. "I could have had my old job as merchandising manager," he says, "but I wanted to run the computer business."

In 1977, RadioShack introduced the first mass-produced personal computer: the TRS-80. Unlike the build-it-yourself units available at the time, the TRS-80, affectionately known as the "Trash 80," was ready to go when the user plugged it in. Although primitive by today's standards, it was a technical breakthrough and an instant hit. With a price tag of $599.99, the TRS-80 Model I included a black-and-

white monitor, a fifty-three-key keyboard, and BASIC.

Tandy, who had projected sales of three thousand units for the first year, was amazed when ten thousand TRS-80s went out the front door. More than two hundred thousand were sold during the four years it was on the market.

"We were soon producing a whole line of computers," Shirley says. "I helped to introduce all of them and ended up managing four manufacturing facilities, an extremely large warehouse, and five thousand employees."

Shirley met Bill Gates in 1978. "He was doing BASIC for us," Shirley says. "Bill and I did a number of products together. The Model 100 was a collaboration among Microsoft, RadioShack, and Kyocera. Bill was involved from day one, and it was the last product that he personally wrote code for."

The Model 100 is considered one of the most important computers in the history of the industry. Priced between $800 and $1,300, it was the first practical, portable laptop and—with its simple editor and built-in modem—was soon a must for the media.

It did have one drawback. The 100's keyboard was extremely noisy, and reporters were often asked to refrain from typing during press conferences because the speaker could not be heard over the clacking keys.

In 1983, when Paul Allen became ill and had to leave Microsoft, Bill Gates found himself running the company, a position for which he was unprepared. Gates asked Shirley if he would consider becoming the president of Microsoft. "RadioShack was Microsoft's largest customer," Shirley says. "I had been in Seattle many, many times, and to the offices in Bellevue, but never really saw anything. I'd get in late, rent a car, get a room, drive to the office in the morning, and leave that night. Our son, Erick, graduated from Lewis and Clark College in 1982. After the graduation, Mary and I went to Seattle and acted like tourists. We drove all over the area and fell in love with the city. So, when I got the offer from Microsoft, the move to Seattle was the easy part. Bill thought we might not be interested and he would really have to fight to get me." Shirley smiles, "Naturally, that allowed me the chance to fight back a little."

The 1956 Ferrari 290MM Scaglietti Spyder. Each cylinder in the 3.5-liter V-12 is fitted with two spark plugs. The juice is provided by two distributors. Shirley purchased this car in pieces in June 1998. The engine was sent to Italy for rebuilding, and the car went to Pete Lovely Racing for restoration. The 290MM has won numerous awards, including both Best of Class and the Luigi Chinetti Trophy for most significant Ferrari at the Pebble Beach Concours in 2001. Shirley, along with his son Peter, drove the car in the 2002 Mille Miglia.

Mark C. Stephens, who wrote for the computer trade magazine *InFo World* under the name, Robert X. Cringely, described Jon Shirley as "the only CEO of Microsoft to be universally identified as a grown-up" and "the person who turned Microsoft into a real company."

During Shirley's tenure, Windows was introduced, Microsoft moved to the Redmond campus, and the company made its initial public offering. "Bill and I had a great relationship," Shirley says. "During the first few months that I was there, we figured out what I'd do and what he'd do. It was very informal. There were times when I would talk to him about something, and other times when I didn't have to talk to him. It worked out well."

Shirley smiles, "If we had a problem to solve, we would usually end up with the same conclusion. If you asked us how we got there, it would be totally different."

Drawing on his experience at RadioShack, Shirley created a business infrastructure that is basically unchanged today. "It was the kind of thing that Tandy had trained me to do," he says. "Hire people, get an organization set up, find the necessary facilities to get the job done, all of that. It was a very interesting time. When I got there, we were a $50 million company with 370 employees. When I left, Microsoft had five thousand employees and was a $1 billion company."

In January 1990, *Business Week* reported that the fifty-one-year-old president of Microsoft had announced his retirement. "I told Bill from the beginning that I was going to retire early if I could," Shirley says. He retired officially on June 30, 1990, but he continues to play a role in the management of Microsoft, both as a member of the board of directors and as a consultant involved with special projects.

I interviewed Shirley on the last day of the 2003 Colorado Grand. He had just parked his 375MM Ferrari, which he and his wife had driven in the event, in Vail Village, where all the cars were on display. At one point I asked him if life was good, or something to that effect. "Yes," he said. "Life is great."

Thinking about it now, Jon and Mary Shirley had just spent four days driving through some of the most magnificent scenery in the United States, in one of the world's most beautiful cars. My question was probably a tad rhetorical.

John Bennett

has worked for Jon Shirley for more than five years, since taking early retirement from AT&T. He explains, "When I first became involved with John, I was just helping him out as a friend. One year we towed one of his Ferraris out to Colorado for the Colorado Grand, and after the event we towed it back to Seattle. One day Jon and I were talking about his car collection and the fact that he needed somebody to help with the cars and the building." Smiling, he says, "I've been around cars all my life, and it was a wonderful opportunity."

Bennett grew up in Seattle. "I was nuts about Ferraris and the cool sounds they made. TVs were scarce in those days, so we read magazines like *Sports Car Graphic* to keep ourselves up to date on the racing scene. Back then, my racing heroes were Juan Fangio, Phil Hill, and, later, Jim Clark."

After high school, Bennett began flagging at local SCCA races. "That kind of racing," he says, is where my roots are. We worked regional and national SCCA events and a few pro races like the TransAm and Continental series. I got to meet Penske, Donahue, and Parnelli Jones. This was back before they had a lot of rules, and you were only five or ten feet away from the track when those guys were ripping by. We had to jump over the bank when Parnelli was driving because he was

This is not Charlie's Body and Paint. The Ferrari 250 GTO at Dennison International Motorsports. During a rallye in France celebrating the GTO's fortieth anniversary, a driver ran into Shirley's car, damaging the front end and left fender. The car was repaired at Butch Dennison's shop and is now back in Shirley's warehouse.

always somewhere out in the dirt." Bennett laughs, "He'd give you the finger if you gave him a passing flag."

During the 1960s Bennett met a fellow who was racing a TransAm Z28 Camaro. "I'd go to his house at night and help him work on the car," he says. "Eventually, I was part of the crew."

After a few years with the Camaro, Bennett decided he wanted to try open-wheel racing. "I managed to get a paying job as the crew chief for a doctor who owned a Formula Ford. I did that for a couple of years, and it was a lot of fun. But, with work and family, I didn't have enough time, so I quit. Over the years, I've kept an interest in racing, but I don't get to the track very often." He shrugs, "There's an endless list of things to be done around here, and I'm kind of finicky when it comes to making things look good."

Bennett's attention to detail is obvious when you visit Shirley's warehouse. Nondescript on the outside, the building's interior is a study in functional minimalism. The old cliché that you could eat off the floor certainly applies here.

A flight of stairs leads to a balcony that provides a bird's-eye view of the collection. The balcony level features a kitchen, a library, and a row of display cases filled with an amazing collection of model Ferraris. The walls, upstairs and on the main floor, are covered with an important collection of posters, photographs, and other ephemera. I was especially impressed by several original technical drawings signed by Enzo Ferrari.

The collection was originally housed in another warehouse, close to the present location, but Shirley decided he wanted something more suited to his needs. The Shirleys are involved in fundraising for a number of organizations, and on occasion they host parties and other events at the garage.

The new building was completed several years ago. "We've been really happy with this building. Our other place had rugs on the floor, and the dust was terrible. The cars had to be dusted every three days. Here, it is once a week.

"But this is not a museum!" Bennett declares, emphatically. "Jon likes to drive his cars, and he expects that they will be ready to go. He will call, for example, and say, 'I want to drive the Cal Spyder today. I'll be there in twenty minutes.' Or, he'll take the XKE for a long drive in the mountains."

To ensure that a car is ready to go, Bennett has put together a book for each one that includes a checklist. "When a car is going to be driven," he says, "I go down the list, making sure that everything is working: brakes, lights, signals, even the horn. All the stuff you normally don't think about." One item that Bennett always checks carefully is the wire wheels. "I always take a big lead hammer and pound away. I want to make sure everything is locked on tight so Jon can get the car back without having a wheel fall off."

Bennett believes it is important to drive the cars on a regular basis. "We drive them," he says, "but not nearly enough. They should be taken out every couple of months to keep them in tip-top shape. Some we drive more than that, but others are driven only two or three times a year."

Most of Bennett's driving is what he calls "Sunday-only driving." Sitting in a traffic jam is not the ideal way to maintain a high-powered collectible car, so he does most of his driving early in the morning. "I like to get them into some twisty situations," he says. "That gets the suspension working and loosened up. I will also do some high-speed freeway driving. Many of these cars, like the Daytona, were made to go fast. You have to take them out once in a while and leg it out. It's quite an experience."

One of three factory mechanic's tool sets, designed by Aurelio Lampredi, that were made in the Ferrari factory to maintain the four- and six-cylinder engines. After working for Piaggio and Isotta Fraschini, Lampredi joined Ferrari in 1946 and designed the 4.5-liter V-12 engine. At the end of his career, he was working for Fiat.

Vinnie Terranova

During the spring of 1903, four young men—Arthur, William, and Walter Davidson, and their next-door neighbor, William Harley—erected a ten-foot-by-fifteen-foot shed in the back of the Davidsons' Milwaukee home. When the building was finished, one of the boys took a paintbrush and proudly printed the name of their new company on the door in block letters—Harley Davidson Motor Co. Although the Davidsons outnumbered Harley, he was given top billing because Harley was the one responsible for the design of Harley-Davidson's first motorcycle. A total of three machines were produced during the company's first year in business, all bought and paid for before they were completed. The first, ridden by a succession of five owners, was featured in a 1912 Harley-Davidson ad. Not only had the motorcycle covered more than 100,000 miles, none of its major components needed to be replaced, and the cycle's engine was still running with its original bearings.

The Davidsons and Harley shared common sense and an old-fashioned work ethic. Talking about those early years, Walter Davidson said, "We worked every day, Sunday included, until at least ten o'clock at night. I remember it was an event when we quit work on Christmas night at eight o'clock to attend a family reunion."

In 1906, the company's first building, financed by a loan from the Davidsons' uncle, was built on the site of Harley-Davidson's original shed. That year, the plant produced fifty Silent Gray Fellows. The *silent* was inspired by the firm's commitment to large mufflers and quiet motorcycling, obviously a tradition that was short-lived. *Gray* was Harley-Davidson's standard color, although black was available as an option. Early riders saw the motorcycle, like the horse it would soon replace, as a companion and friend, hence *fellow*.

From these humble beginnings, Harley-Davidson has become one of the world's most recognizable corporate names and the undisputed "King of the Road" for millions of enthusiasts. Harley-Davidson motorcycles have helped win wars, raced to victory on countless racetracks, survived the Depression and a merger with AMF, chased generations of speeders, become the symbol for rebellious youth, and turned the annual biker rally in Sturgis, South Dakota, into a cultural phenomenon. Under the stewardship of a group of dedicated executives, including Von Beals, Richard Teerlink, and Willy G. Davidson, William Davidson's grandson, the company engineered one of the most spectacular comebacks ever seen in American industry.

What started out at the turn of the century as an attempt to build a dependable means of transportation has turned into an industry with a nearly unrivaled, loyal cult following. Very few products can boast of its customers providing free advertising in the form of tattoos.

In addition to an incredible variety of accessories for customizing and individualizing Harleys, riders can buy all sorts of clothing items to promote the Harley lifestyle. Even Barbie and Ken are available with Harley togs. Bruce Willis, Michael Douglas, and Arnold Schwarzenegger are enthusiastic Harley riders, along with Cher and King Juan Carlos of Spain.

Previous page: Vinny, left, and Troy Terranova with Vinny's custom, old-school Harley-Davidson chopper built with new, high-tech components. Rocky Mountain Harley-Davidson is located in suburban Littleton, south of Denver. The design of the contemporary 30,000-square-foot building's entrance echoes Harley-Davidson's famous V-twin engine. Soaring ceilings and expanses of glass provide a stunning background for Terranova's impressive collection of vintage motorcycles, toys, and memorabilia. The toy motorcycles pictured are all from Terranova's collection.

Above: The "Blade's" first chopper. "It was a 1952 Panhead that I built in 1969," Terranova says. "The bike was a dresser that I bought from an older guy, and I threw away the tank, saddle bags, all that stuff. I'd really love to have those parts today."

Right: Terranova at the Englewood store in 1996. A living endorsement of the biker's creed, "Live to Ride, Ride to Live," Terranova has been a part of a great American success story. After the company's buyout by AMF, Harley-Davidson appeared to be rapidly sinking toward bankruptcy, but a group of investors, including Willie G. Davidson, grandson of founder William A. Davidson, took a gamble and purchased the ailing company in 1981. A combination of revolutionary manufacturing processes, dramatic improvements in quality, and creative marketing restored the "American Legend" to financial stability and renewed excellence.

An unrestored 1916 Harley-Davidson Model F. Powered by Harley-Davidson's trademark forty-five-degree V-twin flathead engine, the bike had a top speed of sixty mph. The "Silent Gray Fellow" featured a chain-drive, three-speed, sliding-gear transmission, a rear drum brake, and an engine-driven oil pump. The "full-floating" passenger

seat, an accessory in 1916, appears to be a rather precarious perch. During 1916, Harley-Davidson motorcycles saw their first military duty in border skirmishes with Pancho Villa. In World War I, more than 20,000 cycles would serve as dispatch and scout vehicles. The majority came from Milwaukee.

Harley-Davidson's comeback has also made savvy investors a great deal of money. Not only have the motorcycle maker's profits constantly exceeded projections, sales are even up in Japan, of all places. Today, 633 dealers sell Harley-Davidson motorcycles in the United States. A Harley-Davidson store is a combination showroom, service center, boutique, gift shop, and clubhouse.

The bikes are expensive, costing upward of $25,000, depending on the model and features. Even if you have the money, you might have to be patient because there are long waiting lists for new bikes. The new model year is essentially sold out before the bikes are even built.

Vinny "The Blade" Terranova is a living endorsement of the biker's creed, "Live to Ride, Ride to Live." Terranova also sells Harley-Davidson motorcycles. His store, Rocky Mountain Harley-Davidson, holds the distinction of being among the company's top ten dealerships worldwide.

Terranova and his ex-wife, Kathy Yevoli, are equal partners in Rocky Mountain Harley-Davidson. Anyone who has any experience with ex-wives or ex-husbands has to be impressed with the relationship they share.

"Kathy does the work behind the scenes," Terranova says, "and we work very well together. We were married when we were young, and things happen. She remarried, I'm remarried, everybody gets along. Life's too short to let a divorce become war."

Above: Walter Davidson Sr., pictured with his single-twin motorcycle, earned a perfect score in his 1908 Endurance Run win. Photograph © Harley-Davidson

Right: A load of new bikes had just arrived at Dudley Perkins's New England Branch. The store opened for business in 1914.

"Vinny is our in-house star," Kathy says. "The personality and philosophy that make Rocky Mountain Harley-Davidson what it is has an awful lot to do with Vinny. I think the two of us work together well as a team because he's the blue sky and I'm the grounder. Even though we are now a major presence in the Harley-Davidson world, Vinny always looks at where we've been and I have to focus on where we're going."

Kathy reaches in a drawer and pulls out a T-shirt. "When Vinny turned fifty, we had these shirts made that say, 'He's a way of life for over 50 years.' I've always felt Vinny's magic. He could be so far out sometimes and I'd say, 'What, are you out of your mind? This isn't going to work!' He'd say, 'Trust me.' Things happen when Vinny's around."

Kathy and Vinny have two boys from their marriage, Troy and Donovan. Vinny also has two boys from his second marriage, Pierre and John Philippe, and Kathy and her husband have a daughter, Marina.

Troy has worked at the dealership since he was fifteen. "When I started, I cleaned bathrooms, emptied trash cans, dumped oil—getting down into it." Now twenty-seven, and "going to college, on and off," Troy runs the service department. "It's a tough job, but I know I'm needed. I enjoy working with people and a product that is exciting. There are those occasional customers who forget that riding a motorcycle is supposed to be fun, but fortunately, out of one hundred customers, ninety-nine of them are a lot of fun."

Growing up with a father who owns a Harley-Davidson dealership held mixed blessings for Troy. "I kind of took it for granted," he says. "Almost to the point where I shied away from it. I'm not what you'd call a biker. Don't get me wrong, I enjoy Harleys, but I've never let it get into my blood like my folks did." As he gets older, however, Troy admits, "I'm beginning to enjoy the mystique of it all."

A 1972 BSA Victor. Designed for hill climbs and off-road racing, the single-cylinder Victor was described by a British magazine as "a real rortin' an' snortin' machine." Other riders, disenchanted with the bike's hard starting, dubbed it "the victim."

W.E. Brough began production of his Brough Superior motorcylces in 1921. The SS100 was introduced in 1922, advertised as the Rolls-Royce of motorcycles." Colonel T.E. Lawrence, better known as Lawrence of Arabia, was a big fan of Brough motorcycles, owning at least seven of them during his lifetime. He was riding a SS100 when he was killed in May 1935. Terranova's SS100 was manufactured in 1938, two years before Brough went out of business. This is the rarest motorcycle in the collection.

Kathy Yevoli remembers when her ex-husband told her he wanted to buy a Harley-Davidson dealership. "His family thought he was out of his mind," she says. Still partners, and best friends, Kathy and Vinny have made it work.

It was very good timing. Denver was in the midst of a building boom, and Lazar was soon doing the majority of the city's large projects. Once again, however, Terranova found himself getting restless. "After five years in Denver," he says, "the construction business wasn't a challenge anymore. I was looking around for something new to try."

One of Terranova's childhood friends, Terry Dunkle, was also looking for a new job. "We go way back," Terranova says. "Terry and I were building choppers when we were in high school. We had stayed in touch, and when he moved to Denver, he went to work for me in the construction business."

Terranova bought his first motorcycle, a 1952 pan head, when he was seventeen. "I always had a love of motorcycles," he says. "I rode them when I was in New York, California, and Denver. They were all Harleys, except for a Triumph Tiger Cub that I used to play with in the dirt."

When he heard about a Harley dealer who was thinking about selling his business, Terranova went to see him. "This was back in the seventies, and the guy looked at me and said, 'What the hell do you know about anything?' I said, 'I'm not sure what I know, but I know I can buy your business.' He told me to come back when I had the money and he'd talk to me."

At that time, there were about 1,100 Harley dealers. The store Terranova was looking at was, as he describes it, "on the end of the line." He says, "In the good old days, they were giving out Harley dealerships to the guy selling John Deere tractors in some little podunk town."

By that time Terranova was married to Kathy, and they had a one-year-old son and another child on the way. Kathy, who grew up in Pennsylvania, recalls the day they met. "He was one of the first people I met in Denver," she says. "I was going for a job interview at an upscale barber shop in downtown Denver, and he held the door for me." She also remembers when Vinny came home and told her he was thinking about buying a Harley dealership. "His family thought he was out of his mind," she says. "Everybody was doing everything they could to discourage him. You don't give up ten years in the union, all that old-school stuff. I said, 'You know what, Vinny? I'm still capable of working. You're young. If it works, it works; if it doesn't, it doesn't.'"

Terranova and Dunkle managed to put together $50,000, and Rocky

Mountain Harley-Davidson opened on February 10, 1979. (To put things in perspective, if you wanted to open a Harley-Davidson dealership today, you would have to have at least $1 million in liquid assets, and then Harley-Davidson might talk to you.)

The late 1970s were difficult years for Harley-Davidson dealers. After the company merged with AMF, quality control became a big problem. "Harley-Davidson was just another one of AMF's companies," Terranova says. "It was also the time when the Japanese were flooding the market with cheap bikes."

Terranova is not totally negative about the AMF years. "They saved Harley-Davidson from going out of business," he says, "and actually they did a few good things. AMF came out with the Super Glide and the alternator motor. They also figured out how to solve the problems we were having with back-ordered parts."

Things, however, were starting to look bleak enough for Harley-Davidson's future that Terranova began to make plans. "I never thought Harley would go away," he says. "Even if the company went out of business, the bikes weren't going to disappear. I was going to get into manufacturing—making parts and buying up old inventory to keep the bikes running."

When the buyout from AMF was announced, Dunkle went to see Kathy. "He talked to me," she says, "before he went to Vinny." Dunkle and his wife thought that Harley-Davidson would expire if the company went out on its own, and they wanted to be bought out. Kathy told him that he had better come up with a figure because she and Vinny had put their whole lives into the business. "We had gambled our house, and Vinny gave up ten years in the union," Kathy says. "I told him we were in this for the long haul."

Kathy was by then doing the dealership's bookkeeping and running the office. "I can tell you honestly," she says, "that

Vinny and I were nervous Nellies for those first few years." To add to their problems, the city condemned their shop, along with several other small businesses, to make room for a mall. "You know," Kathy says. "Good things happen to Vinny. Here we were, still recovering from the buyout of his partner, and all of a sudden we were expected to buy real estate. We lucked into the property on Broadway."

The dealership moved to a new building in Englewood where Rocky Mountain Harley-Davidson would remain until 1999. "It was a 7,000-square-foot store," Terranova says, "and we had seven employees."

"We were soon working a huge business," Kathy says, "out of a very small facility. Those years were very good to Vinny and myself."

It was in the Broadway store that Terranova first began to display his rapidly growing collection of vintage motorcycles and memorabilia. Asked to pick a favorite, Terranova shakes his head. "Picking out a favorite Harley would be like picking which one of my kids I like best. Every one is unique. It depends on what kind of mood you are in because every bike puts you in a different place. Maybe you just want something where there's no work. Grab a new bike and cruise." He points to a very large, very red Harley-Davidson that sports studs on the seat and leather saddlebags. "Or, do you want to ride something that that needs adjusting? Riding that knucklehead is a little bit like riding an old tractor. The bike might even break down and somebody will have to come and get you. But that's all part of the mood you want."

Among the non-Harleys, Terranova admits that he is partial to "my namesake, the Vincent Black Shadow. That is a very neat bike, very fast and unique." Built during the 1950s, the Black Shadow was the fastest production bike in the world at that time.

Hunter Thompson wrote about the Vincent Black Shadow in *Fear and Loathing: On the Campaign Trail '72*: "A genuinely hellish bike. Second gear peaks around 65—cruising speed on the freeways—and third winds out somewhere between 95 and 100. I never got to fourth, which takes you up to 120 or so—and after that you shift into fifth. Top speed is 140, more or less, depending how the thing is tuned—but there is nowhere in Los Angeles County to run a bike like that."

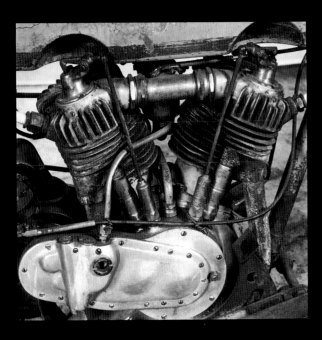

"The motorcycle is a perfect metaphor for the twentieth century. Invented at the beginning of the industrial age, its evolution tracks the main current of modernity. The object and its history represent the themes of technology, engineering, innovation, design, mobility, speed, rebellion, desire, love, sex, and death. For much of society, the motorcycle remains a forbidden indulgence, an object of fascination, fantasy, and anger." Thomas Krens, *The Art of the Motorcycle*

Bruce Weiner

Bruce Weiner opened his first business when he was sixteen. "A friend of mine," he says, "Howard Smuschkowitz, ran a flea market in his father's shopping mall in Toronto. My father was in the automotive aftermarket business: car stereos, alarms, cleaners, stuff like that. He had a warehouse full of products that he had accumulated over the years—samples and lines that he didn't distribute anymore." Weiner, whose parents were divorced, spent the school year in Boca Raton, Florida, with his mother, and summers in Toronto with his father. He laughs, "My father made a deal with me that I'd sell the stuff at the flea market, and we'd split whatever I made, fifty-fifty. That first day, I came home with close to $7,000, and he immediately cut me back to seventy-five–twenty-five."

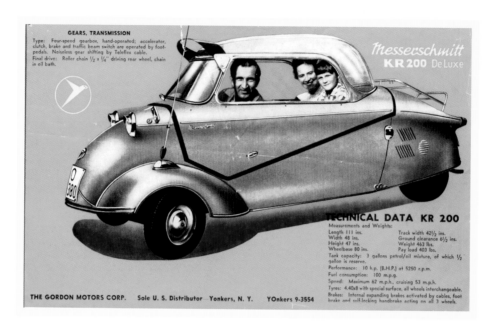

GEARS, TRANSMISSION

Type: Four-speed gearbox, hand-operated; accelerator, clutch, brake and traffic beam switch are operated by foot-pedals. Noiseless gear shifting by Teleflex cable.
Final drive: Roller chain ½ x ¼" driving rear wheel, chain in oil bath.

Messerschmitt
KR 200 DeLuxe

TECHNICAL DATA KR 200
Measurements and Weights:
Length 111 ins.   Track width 42½ ins.
Width 48 ins.   Ground clearance 6½ ins.
Height 47 ins.   Weight 463 lbs.
Wheelbase 80 ins.   Pay load 403 lbs.
Tank capacity: 3 gallons petrol/oil mixture, of which ½ gallon is reserve.
Performance: 10 h.p. (B.H.P.) at 5250 r.p.m.
Fuel consumption: 100 m.p.g.
Speed: Maximum 62 m.p.h, cruising 53 m.p.h.
Tyres: 4.40x8 with special surface, all wheels interchangeable.
Brakes: Internal expanding brakes activated by cables, foot brake and self-locking handbrake acting on all 3 wheels.

THE GORDON MOTORS CORP.   Sole U. S. Distributor   Yonkers, N. Y.   YOnkers 9-3554

He enrolled at Tulane University and majored in business. "After I graduated," he says, "I moved to Toronto and went to work for my father. That lasted six months."

Weiner called his old friend Howard and told him that he wanted to set up in the flea market. "I bought fifty reproduction antique gumball machines with my American Express card," he says. "I didn't have a clue how I was going to pay for them, but luckily, I sold out the first day."

Impressed, Smuschkowitz wanted to open a store and sell the gumball machines, but Weiner was thinking much bigger than that. "I told Howard," he says, "I don't want a store, I want to distribute the machines. We formed a partnership, Concord Confections, and started importing the machines from Taiwan and selling them to K-Mart, Woolco, Sears, all the big chain stores. The experience helped sharpen my business skills because dealing with the Taiwanese manufacturers was tough. They haggled over every fraction of a cent."

After six years, Weiner and Smuschkowitz added a third partner, Serge Nussbaum. "Howard and I," Weiner says, "had always compared the gum machines

and gum to cameras and film. Cameras may change, but you always need film. The machines were just a fad, but gum is forever. Serge knew how to make gum."

Weiner's mother actually found Nussbaum. "Serge," Weiner says, "lived in Montreal and was visiting his relatives in Florida. He met my mother, and, when she found out he knew how to make gum, she told Nussbaum, 'You should talk to my son, he wants to make his own gum.' I put his number on my bulletin board, called him six months later, and a week later we made a deal."

With Nussbaum aboard, Concord Confections began to manufacture its own brand of gum, Kid Gumball. "We began to add other products," Weiner says, "and when Fleer, the company that made Double Bubble, came up for sale through the Marvel Entertainment bankruptcy, we bought Fleer. I'm vice-president for sales and marketing, and this year we will do over $100 million selling gum."

Weiner began to collect English sports cars after he moved to Toronto. "I always liked cars," he says, "and I put together a rather eclectic collection. I had an Austin Healey, a Jaguar XKE, an MGB, and a couple of Triumphs, but I also had a Ferrari and a Porsche. At one point I bought a Model T Ford just to try it out."

Previous page: Peter Svilans exercises a 1955 Messerschmitt KR-200. Topped with a large plastic aircraft-style dome, the Messerschmitt Kabinenroller—the first bubble car—developed from designer Fritz Fend's desire to build a vehicle for disabled World War II veterans. The combination of Messerschmitt's name and the bubble top gave rise to the legend that the cars were built from leftover fighter plane parts. They were not.

Above: A happy German family in their KR-200 Deluxe Messerschmitt. After World War II, much of Europe, England, and Japan lay in ruins. With money, manufacturing facilities, and gasoline in short supply, a group of innovative designers reinvented the automobile for those austere times.

Right: A design by Gabriel Voisin. During the 1940s, Voisin's company was taken over by engine builders Gnome and Rhone. Between 1949 and 1953, Voisin utilized his knowledge of aircraft construction to design a series of minimalist vehicles called Biscooters. This unique example, built in 1952, seats four and features circular doors. Conflicts between Voisin and the directors of the company resulted in the sale of the license in June 1953 to Spain's Autonacional SA, which renamed the car Biscuter and went on to build 20,000 examples.

Peel Engineering Limited was located on the Isle of Man. In 1962, the firm introduced the Peel P50, the world's smallest car. Problems, including the tiny vehicle's propensity for rolling over when cornering, plagued the P50. The Trident was developed in 1966. Seating two, the futuristic fiberglass body shell was topped by a large, clear plastic dome that lifted for entry. Power was provided by a 98cc engine used in Triumph Tina scooters. A 1965 review in *Scooter and Three Wheeler* magazine found that "the motor was as lively as a cricket." A brochure bragged about the Trident's "Armchair Seating" and "Saloon Car Comfort." I managed to stuff myself into Weiner's Trident and found neither.

His work during the war had given Fend access to many German aircraft manufacturers, including Willi Messerschmitt. Messerschmitt, a larger-than-life aeronautical genius, opened his first factory in 1923 at the age of twenty-three. He went on to design many of the Third Reich's most formidable fighter planes, including the menacing Bf. 109, the Me 162 Komet rocket-powered interceptor, and the Me 262 Schwalbe (Swallow), the first jet fighter to fly in combat.

Almost 75 percent of Messerschmitt's Augsburg works had been bombed into ruins, and the terms of Germany's surrender prohibited the firm from building airplanes. After five years of difficult rebuilding, Messerschmitt was producing electric sewing machines and auto parts. When Fend approached Messerschmitt with a proposal that they combine forces to build an enclosed scooter, the ex-aircraft builder was not only willing to build the cars, but also agreed to lend his name to the project.

Fend spent the next year developing a new machine, and the KR-175 Kabinenroller debuted at the Geneva Automobile Show in March, 1953. Standing only forty-seven inches high, the three-wheeled car's frame, like the Flitzer's, was constructed from steel tubing, combined with an all-steel, monocoque body, a method of construction not unlike that found in modern race cars. The body was topped with a large, plastic aircraft-style dome—the first bubble car.

The fuselage-style body, tandem seating, and clear canopy, along with the Messerschmitt label, gave rise to the myth that the cars were built from leftover fighter-plane parts, a misconception that still occasionally appears in print. The KR-175 was entered by lifting the plastic top, hinged on the right side. One writer described entering a Messerschmitt "as one does a bath—one leg at a time." The driver sat in front, passenger behind. The front wheels were steered with chrome-plated, cycle-style handlebars complete with a twist-grip throttle. There was no

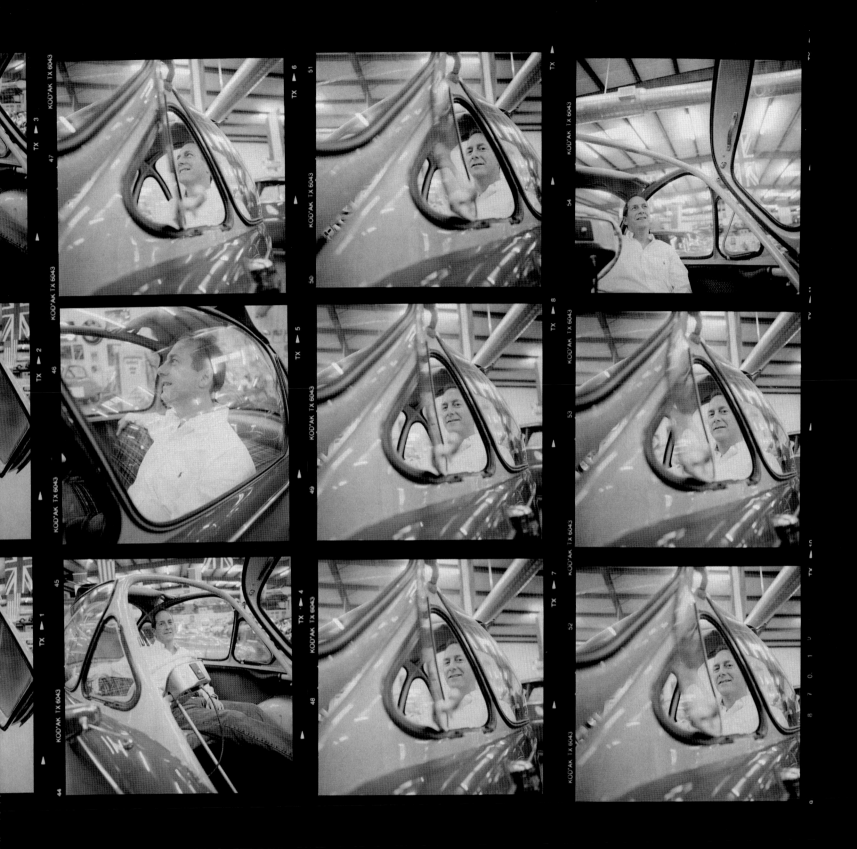

Bruce Weiner photographed in a 1963 Trojan 200. When Aircraft designer Ernst Heinkel decided he could build a better Isetta, he designed the Kabine 150. A cross between the Messerschmitt and Isetta, the car sold well, but the company lost money. When Heinkel was once again allowed to produce aircraft, he wanted the cars to go away. A license was awarded to produce the cars in Argentina and Ireland. Shoddy workmanship resulted in the Irish license being revoked, and it was given to Trojan, an English company known for its rugged utility vehicles. The Trojan was produced until 1966, giving it the distinction of being the longest-surviving bubble car.

A 1957 Jurish Motoplan. Motorcyclist Carl Jurish was convinced that the future of transportation lay in a personal single-seat vehicle. Jurish used a widened motorcycle sidecar as the body for his Jurish Motoplan, powered by a one-cylinder motor-scooter engine. At one point Jurish brought the car to the offices of *Das Motorrad* magazine, but the editors refused to test it, asking him, "Who would buy such a silly impractical thing?" In conjunction with a motorcycle dealer, Jurish tried to market the tiny car in New York City; unfortunately, it was a time when Americans were thinking "bigger is better." Only three cars were built. This is the only known survivor.

clutch pedal, as the clutch was automatically actuated by the gear lever. A single-cylinder 174cc engine, producing nine horsepower, gave the car a top speed of somewhere around 50 mph—depending on which way the wind was blowing.

The Kabineroller, despite some teeth-rattling suspension troubles, was an instant success, and nearly 20,000 were built during the two years it was produced. The car was especially popular with motorcycle and scooter riders who were tired of riding their machines in inclement weather. Priced at 2,375

Deutschmarks ($475), the Messerschmitt was positioned between a Vespa scooter (1,500 DM), and an NSU Prinz minicar (3,800 DM). This put the little machine within the budget of the vast majority of Europeans, who at that time could not afford a conventional automobile.

After a lengthy development period, the much-improved and more civilized KR-200 was introduced in 1955. Power was increased to 10.5 horsepower. The agricultural ride of the 175 was tamed by shock absorbers, and the engine's

Prototypes of the Fuldamobil N-2 had wooden bodies covered in vinyl and were powered by chainsaw engines. On later models, additional power was provided by a 359cc single-cylinder engine, and the vinyl was replaced with hammered sheet aluminum. This prompted the nickname "Silver Flea." In 1956, formed aluminum panels replaced the wood, and the car was equipped with two rear wheels. The Fuldamobil is among the longest-built microcars, but in the car's nearly twenty-year run, a mere 3,000 examples were produced. Weiner's example is a 1953 N-2, powered by a single-cylinder engine producing 9.5 horsepower.

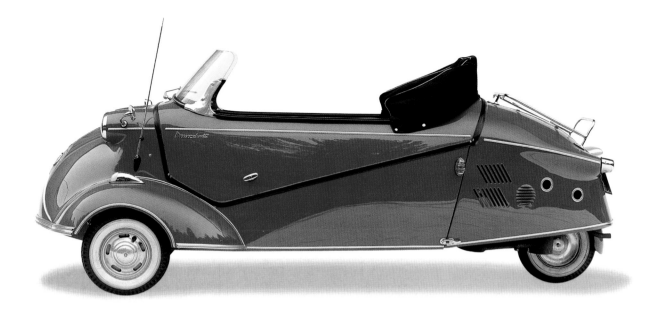

The Messerschmitt KR-201 Roadster was introduced on June 24, 1957. The car featured a folding roof, signal red paint, snakeskin trim, and redesigned headlight, mirrors, and hubcaps. A one-cylinder Fichtel & Sachs two-stroke engine put out 10 horsepower. Although the convertible top solved the problem of the sun beating down on the Plexiglas canopy, the flexible, clear plastic side curtains left a lot to be desired. Not only were they extremely awkward to use, they also leaked. Only 300 of the stylish little three-wheeled Roadsters were built. Weiner's KR-201 is one of twenty-one that have survived.

vibrating buzz was smoothed by rubber motor mounts. A wider back seat could accommodate an additional child or a piece of luggage. Although the handlebars were retained, the controls were more carlike, and two-tone paint was an option. More than 30,000 KR-200s were built.

In 1957 the ban on aircraft production in Germany was lifted, and Willi Messerschmitt wanted out of the automobile business. In conjunction with Knott, the company that was building the brakes for the cars, Fritz Fend set up his own company, Fahrzeng und Maschinenbau Regensburg (FMR), to produce the cars. The new company was allowed to continue using the Messerschmitt name, but without the aircraft company's Augsburg Eagle badge.

To address the problem of heat under the canopy, a convertible roadster was introduced. The KR-201 looked spectacular, but the waterproofing qualities of the snap-in, clear vinyl side-curtains were less than satisfactory. This model was followed a year later by the Cabriolet, a much more practical soft-top car with fixed frames

In 1947, Robert Hannoyer, owner of a car repair shop in Paris, developed a car that he thought would solve the problems of urban driving. The two-seat car, called the Reyonnah (Hannoyer backward), was equipped with a front suspension that allowed the front wheels to fold downward so that the vehicle could occupy a parking space only 75 cm wide. However, the car was unsuccessful. Its lack of doors made it necessary to climb over the side to get into the car, and the front suspension lacked a lock to keep it in the "up" position, causing it to collapse back to "down" when the car was moved. Weiner's Reyonnah was built in 1951.

swamp, just sinking into the earth. They were so rough that it took me three or four visits before I broke down and bought one of his cars. But it was great fun tromping around in the bush discovering rusted hulks and digging them out like an archaeologist."

Weiner was by then well aware of the restoration magic that Svilans could perform. "As long as a car is original," Weiner says, "and it isn't completely rusted out, Peter can do something with it. When I first started collecting, I would give him the worst cars to do first because I couldn't stand looking at them."

Weiner married Jeanene Thomas in 1988, and they had two children, Brittany and Brandon. The family moved from Toronto to Atlanta in the early 1990s. A true

Southern belle, Jeanene had roots deep in Georgia and never got used to the Canadian winters.

Now that he was commuting between Atlanta and Toronto, Weiner was becoming disenchanted with his car collection. "I wasn't enjoying the cars anymore," he says. "There were forty-four cars sitting in an industrial building in Toronto, I had four people working on them, and it seemed that all I was doing was spending money. Everything was getting so expensive," he continues. "I'd buy a car for $1,000 and end up spending $30,000 to restore it. If I tried to sell it, I didn't think I would ever get my money back. I began thinking to myself, 'this is madness.' A hobby should be an enjoyment, and I was not enjoying it anymore,

The Inter, designed by a group of French aircraft builders, was introduced at the 1953 Paris Auto Show. Available at first only as a single-seater, a two-seater tandem was introduced in 1954. It originally had a folding front suspension like the Reyonnah, but that feature was quickly eliminated. Sideways movement of the gear lever engaged the clutch. The car had a helicopter-type starter, or Gyrostarter, which revved up with a whining sound. When the driver slammed down a lever, the engine engaged and, hopefully, started. This Inter 175 A Berline is a 1955 model.

because for the last few years it had become a business."

Weiner contacted a collector in California and offered him the entire collection. "He was a rather odd fellow," Weiner says. "He'd spend an entire week in Toronto and then come to see me an hour before he had to leave. It turned out that all he wanted were the restored cars."

When that deal fell through, Weiner contacted Christie's auction house in London. "I went to England," Weiner says, "for two reasons. First, I didn't think Americans would buy the cars, and second, I wanted to see them back in Europe, where they were built."

After breaking the news to Svilans, Weiner had everything shipped to London. "When I say everything," Weiner says, "I mean everything. The cars, toys, models, it all went. I didn't want to cherry-pick anything. Once you start doing that, where would you draw the line?"

He laughs, "Oh, I take that back. I couldn't bring myself to part with a '56 Messerschmitt KR-200 that's still in my office in Toronto."

Christie's told Weiner that they wanted to offer his cars in an independent auction. He frowns, "I was afraid no one was going to show up if my cars were the only items for sale. I asked them to please include my cars in a mixed sale. I wasn't expecting to make a profit or even cover my costs. I just wanted to sell them all at one time to avoid having to run a used-microcar dealership."

In 1957, Willi Messerschmitt, like Ernst Heinkel, wanted out of the automobile business so he could return to building airplanes. Fritz Fend, in conjunction with Knott, the company that was building the brakes for the cars, set up his own company, F.M.R., to produce Messerschmitts. Although the new company was allowed to continue using the Messerschmitt name, it could no longer use the aircraft company's Augsburg Eagle badge. A new badge was created, consisting of three rings and the letters "FMR." However, the continued use of old stock explains why this totally original 1958 KR-200 sports the original badge and trim style.

The auction, held on March 6, 1997, included "Important Collectors' Motor Cars, Related Automobilia and Motoring Art, and the Bruce Weiner Microcar Collection." Weiner's fears turned out to be unfounded.

"More than one thousand people showed up, and Christie's sold everything," he says, now smiling. "The restored cars went for very stupid money, and I ended up making $1 million."

The day after the auction, Weiner flew back to Atlanta. Somewhere over the Atlantic Ocean he was stricken with a major case of seller's regret. "The next day," he says, "I called a friend of mine in Germany and told him I wanted to buy some cars. I'm not kidding! I had a six-car garage, and I told him I wanted six perfectly restored cars: a Messerschmitt, an Isetta, a Goggomobil, one French car, one Italian car, and an extra German car. I ended up buying nine cars."

A few weeks later, Weiner bought a farm near Madison, a small, antebellum town about one hundred miles east of Atlanta. "I wanted a place where my family could spend weekends," he says. "But I also realized that I was collecting again, and I needed a place to keep the cars."

In 1999 Weiner went to Germany to attend the microcar meet held every other year in Story. It is considered the premier event for fans of the diminutive vehicles. While there, he visited the Roller and Kleinwagen Museum (devoted to motor scooters and small automobiles), located in Bad Iburg. The museum was run by Manfred Kanuper and his wife. Weiner had purchased cars from Kanuper in the past and told Manfred that he was once again in the market for cars.

Kanuper explained to Weiner that none of his cars were for sale because he was going to have his own auction. "My auction," Weiner says, "had wreaked havoc in the microcar hobby. I was considered a bad guy for having the auction, an evil businessman for making so much money. I was also immoral for getting those people to pay such exorbitant prices. My critics seem to forget the fact that all of my cars were offered without a reserve."

After Kanuper told Weiner about his planned auction, Weiner asked him if he wanted to sell his entire museum and save himself a lot of trouble. Kanuper thought for a minute and quickly said yes.

"I walked around the museum for five minutes," Weiner says, "counting the number of scooters and cars. I figured out what I thought they were worth and told him that I would give him 1 million marks for everything. Within

five minutes, we shook hands and made a deal."

Weiner made it clear to Kanuper that he was buying the entire museum. "Everything," Weiner says. "I told him, don't tell me this belongs to my brother-in-law, or this is my favorite car."

Within forty-five days Kanuper closed the museum, and two months later Weiner sent someone over to Europe to pack everything up. "It filled up eighteen containers," Weiner says. "Manfred had forty-six cars, two hundred scooters, and a lot of other stuff—push cars, pedal cars, irons, sewing machines, cameras, alarm clocks, and toys. I sold off many things, including some duplicate cars, and ended up with thirty vehicles."

Today, the Bruce Weiner Microcar Museum, the world's largest collection of

microcars, numbering more than 175, is housed in a 15,000-square-foot building on his farm, known as Double Bubble Acres, an hour's drive from Atlanta. The only livestock on the farm is, appropriately, a collection of miniature animals.

Accepting his "disease" as terminal, Weiner is in the process of planning a second building, a duplicate of the first. In addition to the cars, his collection includes an awesome compilation of models, toys, advertising, posters, point-of-purchase pieces, and a comprehensive reference library of books and literature—anything and everything to do with microcars.

Working on this book, William and I have had the opportunity to see many of the most important automobiles ever produced. After a while it is easy to become jaded. 'Oh, look, William, it's another Duesenberg SJ, Packard Caribbean, Bugatti, Ferrari, McLaren, or Pierce-Arrow. How nice. Ho hum.' I'm exaggerating, of course, but you get the idea.

Weiner's cars are different. Many are cute, some are peculiar, and more than a few are stone ugly. But, like puppies or babies, you have to love all of them. They were built and driven for little more than a decade, but these unique vehicles provided, in their own modest fashion, valid transportation for those who had no other options.

"Microcars are fun to drive," Weiner says, "because you know you are going to have fun no matter what happens. I have always said that not having any expectations in terms of technology puts you in a different mindset when you drive one of these cars. When I was driving Triumphs, Jaguars, and Porsches, it was extremely upsetting when something went wrong. If it wasn't the fuel pump, it was the clutch, water pump, or wipers. You expect a lot from those cars."

He continues, "When I take a Messerschmitt or a Kleinschnittger to a car show, it won't be long before there will be more people around it than the nicest Ferrari at the meet. People just love these little cars."

Lawrence Bond and his wife collaborated to build a vehicle that would bridge the gap between motorcycle and car. A hole had to be cut through the Bonds' second floor so the prototype could be lowered to the ground. Early Bond Mark As were primitive, but improvements were quick in coming. By the time the Model F was announced in 1958, the car was available in three models, including a four-seat family sedan with a fiberglass roof and two inward-facing hammock seats. This car, painted in the original metallic green and sporting stylish white walls, is a 1950 Mk A.

Acknowledgments

● Dedicated to Barbara Hopke, who has heard these stories at least three times, and Gil Nickel, who I would have liked to have known better.

● I would like to thank the collectors who allowed William and myself to poke around their inner sanctums. Without their cooperation and interest this book would not have happened. It was a pleasure to spend time with them and their extraordinary automobiles, motorcycles, and airplanes. ● The curators and mechanics who maintain the collections were extremely helpful, often going beyond the call of duty—wielding jumper cables and starting fluid to bring reluctant engines to life, wiping off fingerprints, filling flat tires, and moving very large and heavy cars around until the angle and light were perfect. Thanks to Adrian Ayres, John Bennett, Anthony Campoy, Chris Chesbrough, Jesus Gonzales, Greg Jacobs, Keith Lowden, Ron Posey, William Raynor, Juan Roldan, Ed Shura, Peter Svilans, and George Widich. ● Not only is William Taylor a talented photographer, he is also an amiable traveling companion. William is also able to cope with just about any situation. With few exceptions, he had to walk into a collection that neither of us had seen before and capture it on film. Automobiles are difficult to photograph under the best of conditions, and he came through beautifully. As an added benefit, William also brought me up-to-speed on Great Britain, the people who live there, the glory of Lotus, and the finer points of Formula 1. ● Speaking of talent, I have always admired Tom Bentkowski's ability to bring intelligence and beauty to the printed page. For *Wheels*, Tom has used his exceptional skills to create a format that perfectly complements my words and William's photographs. ● Bruce Wennerstrom believed in the project from the beginning. In addition to sharing his formidable automotive and publishing expertise, Bruce allowed me access to his complete collection of *Automobile Quarterly*, for which I am especially indebted to him. ● Eric Himmel, editor-in-chief at Harry N. Abrams, Inc., not only agreed to produce the book, he kept it on track through the usual long and arduous process. Elisa Urbanelli also kept things under control in her graceful manner and provided the skillful and necessary editing. ● Also, special thanks to Larry Bell, Shelly Bennett, Jim Bennett, Tor Brook, Dr. Dick Buckingham, Dan Colberg, Mary Grace at Far Niente, Eric Halborg, Ron Lazar, Sam Meredith, Natalie Pray, Lilly Pray, Pat Ryan, Joe Simpson, Chris Stames for his encyclopedic knowledge of things automotive, Jo Taylor, Wayne Valero for the use of his Cussler archives, Genia Wennerstrom, and Robert Wood.